This Book Is About Time

Marilyn Burns

Illustrated by Martha Weston

Little, Brown and Company

Boston   Toronto   London

This Brown Paper School book was edited and prepared
for publication at the Yolla Bolly Press, Covelo, California,
in the winter and spring of 1978. The series is under the
supervision of James and Carolyn Robertson. Production
staff: Gene Floyd, Loren Fisher, Jay Stewart, Joyca Cunnan,
and Diana Fairbanks.

HC: 10 9 8 7 6 5 4   BP
PB: 10 9 8 7   BB

Published simultaneously in Canada by
Little, Brown & Company (Canada) Limited.
Printed in the United States of America.

Library of Congress Cataloging in Publication Data

Burns, Marilyn.
      This book is about time.

      (A brown paper school book)
      1. Time — Juvenile literature. I. Weston, Martha.
II. Title.
QB209.5.B87   529   78-6614
ISBN 0-316-11752-8
ISBN 0-316-11750-1 pbk.

This book is for the tortoise,
the hare, and anyone else
who has ever had a run-in with time.

What's in this book

Introduction
Starting on Time

When did you last think about time?
Probably either when you were late for
something or looking forward to something. Even though you may never
think much about time, it influences
all parts of your life. Yet time is a funny
thing. Sometimes, a minute can pass un-
noticed. At other times, it can drag on
endlessly.

Got a Minute?

Here's a small idea about time: one minute. People talk about a minute as if
it's not any time at all. They say things
like: "Wait a minute," or "I've only got
a minute," or "I'll be there in a minute."

Just how long is a minute, anyway?
Think about things you do in about one
minute. Brush your teeth? Drink a glass
of water? Write your name a dozen
times? Say the alphabet backwards? Pick
something you think takes you a minute to do. Now stop reading, try it,
and time yourself.

How close were you to estimating one minute accurately? If your estimate was way off, then you need to keep reading this book. You could use some time help for sure. If your estimate was just about right, then you definitely need to keep reading this book. You've got some time talent that shouldn't be wasted.

Getting on with Time

This book is a collection of ways to look at and think about time. There are ways to explore time by yourself, experiments to do with a friend, things to investigate out in the world, and interesting timely information to ponder.

You can learn about how time is changing in our jet age and how that doesn't matter at all to the fiddler crab. You can learn about special time rhythms all around the world, even in your own body. You can find out who has the right time, anyway. You'll be able to make clocks to measure time yourself. You'll explore different ways to split a second. And you'll find much more.

You can read this book one section at a time, or you can take time out from the other things you do and read it all at once. This book can help you pass the time of day. It can give you something to do when you feel like killing a little time or when you've got some time on your hands.

Chapter 1
Warm-Up Time

Here are some beginning time exercises. They're a collection of warm-ups so you can look at how time works in your life and how you use time in different ways. You can do some of these exercises alone. Some work better with a friend or with your family.

Try these time warm-ups before you plunge into the rest of the book. They'll help you to wind up and set your own head so it's ready for what's to come.

What Kind of a Clock Watcher Are You?

What do you use watches and clocks for? That's an easy question, isn't it? Maybe even a dumb one, you might be thinking. You use watches and clocks to tell the time, right? Right.

So far, so good. Now, what do you need to tell the time for? That question may also seem like an easy one or maybe dumb too. But read on a little before you answer.

When do you really need to know what the time is? Do you need a clock to tell you when you're hungry? Some people think they do. They eat supper when it's 6 p.m. and their bodies just better have an appetite then.

Do you need a clock to tell you when it's your bedtime, or do you wait for your body to tell you that it's getting tired and would love to stretch out in bed? Maybe you wait until your parents tell you it's bedtime, no matter what your body feels.

Do you need a clock to tell you that it's time to watch your favorite TV show or time to do your homework or time to get home? Do you need a clock to know when it's leaving-for-school time?

Get a piece of paper. Make a list of at least ten different reasons why you check a clock or watch during the day.

TIME TO LET THE TRAIN THROUGH THE HOUSE.

ALREADY ?

What's Your Daily Time-Check Count?

How many times during a day do you think you look at a clock or watch to check the time? Five? Ten? Nineteen? Thirty-seven? Make a quick guess.

Now try a more careful estimate of how many times you really do check. Think about a usual day — a school day, for instance. Start by thinking about when you get up. Do you look at a clock then? What do you usually do next? Keep count as you think about all the times during the day you most likely check a clock or watch, all the way until you go to bed at night. Jot this estimate down, so you won't forget it.

There's one way to find out more accurately how often you really do check the time: keep track for a day. It's not easy because looking at a clock or watch is an automatic thing for many people to do and so we don't notice we're even doing it. But it's interesting to try, anyway.

Set up a chart on an index card or a piece of paper, like the one shown here, and carry it around with you during the day. Every time you catch yourself checking a clock or watch, write down that time and the reason you checked. After doing this for a day, count up how many time checks you made. How does that compare with your estimate?

Save this list. There are some more activities in this chapter when you'll use it.

TIMES I CHECKED	WHAT I WAS DOING
7:05	WAKING UP
8:10	SEEING IF IT WAS TIME TO GO

The Two Faces of Time

Time appears in your life in two different ways. One is when you're thinking about *interval*. Interval means how long something takes. When you're thinking about how long it will be until dinner, you're thinking about interval.

When you wonder how long a movie or TV show will last or how long your next school vacation will be, that's interval.

But if you're thinking about exactly what time something will happen, then you're thinking about a different kind of time. This is called *epoch*, a location in time. You're thinking about epoch when you wonder what time dinner will be or what time the TV show or movie starts or what day vacation will end.

HEY MOM! HOW MUCH LONGER DO I HAVE TO DO THIS?

INTERVAL OR EPOCH?

These are two very different ways of thinking about time, but you use the same units to measure them — minutes, hours, days. Can you think of times during the day when you use one or the other of these two time ideas? Which do you think you use more often?

Check back over your clock-watching list and see how many of your time checks were for intervals and how many were for epochs.

How Important Is Accurate Time?

When you check the time during a day, what do you usually want to know — the exact time or only about what time it is? You may want the exact time when you need to catch the school bus or to get home in the afternoon or to take the cookies out of the oven. But you may only need the approximate time when you want to know how long it is until dinner or if you have time to get to the store before it closes.

Thinking about this will be easier if you look over that list of time checks you wrote down for a day. Put a small X next to those times it was important to be exact. How many did you mark? What does this tell you about exact time in your life?

Clock Counting

How many clocks are there in your house, not including people's watches? Is there one in every room? More than one in some? None in others? Take a clock count. While you're at it, check to see if all the clocks have the same time.

Time Talk

Time pops up in your life in other ways besides clock checking. The word slips into what people say in lots of different ways. Here are two Time Talk games you can play with just one other person or with a whole group. Both games are ways to explore how people talk about time. Whenever your family has some time on its hands or you're together with one friend or a few friends, try these. Follow the directions first for either of the two games.

Step one. Collect the materials you'll need: a small note pad or twenty-five to thirty index cards, a pencil or pen, and a watch with a second hand.

Step two. Think of all the sayings you can that have the word *time* in them. Whenever someone comes up with one, write it on some notepaper or an index card, so each saying is on its own piece of paper.

Step three. After you've got your collection of sayings, check this list for some ideas you might have missed.

IN THE NICK OF TIME
TIME FLIES
TIME MARCHES ON
TIME ON MY HANDS
A STITCH IN TIME SAVES NINE
TIME OUT
TIME IN
PASSING THE TIME OF DAY
DOING TIME
KILLING TIME
WASTING TIME
LOSING TIME
BEATING TIME
ON TIME
FOR THE TIME BEING
FROM TIME TO TIME
TIME'S UP
THE BIG TIME
TIME IS MONEY
ONCE UPON A TIME
THE TIME OF YOUR LIFE

Step four. Once you've got your collection of time sayings, you're ready to play either or both of the games.

Time Talk Number One: This is a time version of charades. If there are just two of you playing, follow these rules:

1. Take turns.

2. When it's your turn, without looking, pick a time saying from the collection.

3. Tell the other person when you're ready to go so they can check the watch for the starting time and say "Go."

4. Then, without talking or making any noise, act out the idea of the card so that the other person can guess which saying you picked.

5. Score one point if you can get the other person to guess within two minutes.

More than two, follow these rules:

1. Divide into two teams.

2. Without looking, a player from one team picks a saying, and when that person is ready, he or she gives it to the other team.

3. A timekeeper on the other team says "Go."

4. Then, without saying anything, the player tries to act out the saying for his or her team.

5. When the team has guessed correctly, the timekeeper writes the time it took.

6. After everyone has had a turn, add up the times and see which team clocked the least time. That team is the winner.

Sometimes people use time to measure distances. Maybe you've done this for yourself. Have you ever said something like, "I live an hour from my grand-mother," or "I live just ten minutes from school"? Is time a handy way to measure distances?

Time Talk Number Two: This game is especially fun if you like to draw. You'll need some notebook-size paper and pencils for each player. The players pick one or more sayings, whichever they want, and they each draw a picture to illustrate the sayings they've chosen. After everyone has finished drawing, number the drawings. Then each person takes another piece of paper and, looking at the numbered drawings, writes what saying they think the drawing illustrates. Talking about the drawings afterwards will give you an idea if you all agree on what these Time Talk sayings really mean.

Chapter 2
It's Not the Same Time Everywhere

You may already know that it's not the same time everywhere, especially if you have a relative who lives someplace far away. When a very long, long distance telephone call is made, you have to figure time in two places, since it's not the same time where you are and where the other person is.

You may have learned a bit about this in school — about how the earth spins on its axis. When the side of the earth where you live is away from the sun, it is nighttime for you. When the side of the earth where you live is facing the sun, it's daytime. Even though people usually say that the sun is rising or the sun is setting, it's not the sun that is moving. The earth is doing the spinning.

When the sun is most directly overhead, it is midday. That's when the shadows of things are the shortest. There just isn't any way for the sun to be overhead for everyone on the earth at the same time. When it's noon in Chicago, it already was noon in Boston or Miami a while ago, and it won't be noon in California for a couple of hours yet.

Sun Time

In many towns and cities, up to about one hundred years ago, the sun was the official timekeeper. People set their clocks by the sun. It was the old eye-squint method. You checked the sun by eye, and when you figured it was at its peak position, you set your clock or watch to noon. Often jewelers kept clocks outside their stores or in the window so people could see the time and check their watches. But jewelers used the sun too. No two jewelers agreed exactly on when the sun was directly overhead; they might be as much as twenty minutes off from each other. But this system seemed reasonable. Being exact wasn't so important for most people then.

People don't usually use the sun to set their watches today. They use the radio or the telephone or someone else's time. Do these methods help people keep more accurate time now or do people's watches still differ? If they do differ, do they differ as much as the jewelers' clocks often did or just by a few minutes?

How Exact Are People's Times Today?

This experiment will help you find out how accurate people's times are. What you need to do is to ask ten people what time it is according to their watches. The supermarket is a good place to do this. There's usually a collection of people there you can easily ask.

Before you go, prepare a way to keep track of the times you get. An index card is good to use for jotting down the times people tell you. You need a watch, too, so you can mark down your own time right before asking the first person and right after asking the tenth.

Here's a hint. When you're doing the experiment, ask the people as quickly as possible so you don't waste too much time between each one. It helps to check

people's wrists first to see if they're wearing watches at all before you ask. But do this courteously, so you don't seem like some kind of weird kid with a thing about wrists.

Another hint. You need to get the exact time on the person's watch for your experiment. People with digital watches have no choice but to tell you what the numbers say. But it's easy for a person with a regular watch face to say, "Just about five past," rather than saying, "It's 4:06."

You can avoid this problem by telling the person first that you're trying an experiment. Like this: "Excuse me, but I'm doing an experiment about time. Could you please tell me exactly what time your watch has now?" Or you could say: "Excuse me, I'm doing an experiment about time. Could I look at your watch and see exactly what time it says?" This second possibility is good for people who might have trouble reading their own watches without their glasses.

When you've collected all your time statistics, check your results. Since some time is used up between each person asked, the first time on the list should be the earliest, and the tenth should be the latest if everyone is on time. All the rest of the times should be very close, either the same as the one before or after it — or a bit later if it's farther down on the list. All the times should also be in between your own starting and ending times. Do you think you will get these results?

Try it. See if people do keep more accurate time today than people did when they used sun time.

The Railroad Mess

The people who ran the railroads in the middle 1800s found that sun time was no fun. Sun time caused an absolute mess for both the railroad officials and the people who used the railroads for transportation. Being twenty minutes off on your watch is more than enough time to miss a train. Besides, when the railroad schedule was set, the time the railroad officials used wasn't much help if it was different from the local time you used where you lived. It was really awful.

Finally a solution was suggested. It was made by H. S. Pritchett, who was an astronomy professor at Washington University in St. Louis. He realized that it was ridiculous for each person in a town or city to keep his or her own time. What was needed, he thought, was a way for there to be an official time.

His solution was to have a "time ball" in each town and city. He suggested that a large, hollow, metal ball — over a meter in diameter — be fastened to a high pole so it could travel up and down. The ball could be painted red so it would be seen for several miles. Every day, just before noon, the ball could be elevated to the top of the pole. Exactly at noon, it was to be dropped. People on the streets could stop just before noon and keep their eyes on the ball so they could set their watches.

This seemed like a helpful idea, and lots of cities decided to use it, but there was a hitch. Everybody in a particular town now agreed on the time, but it wasn't possible to see the ball from city to city or from town to town. So it still didn't help the railroad people very much.

Here's how bad the mess was. In Michigan, there were twenty-seven local times used in different parts of the state. In Wisconsin, there were thirty-eight. There were twenty-seven different times used in Illinois and twenty-three in Indiana. Each was the sun time for that town.

The different railroad companies each decided to pick one official time to use. But all the companies didn't pick the same official time. In the train station in Buffalo, New York, there were three clocks on the wall. One was set to New York City time. That was the time the New York Central Railroad chose to use. One clock was set to Columbus, Ohio, time, which the Lake Shore and Michigan Southern Railroad used. The third was the local Buffalo time. Can you imagine what it would be like to have the job of making railroad schedules with this situation? You'd have to make a schedule that would tell people what time their train was due to arrive or leave according to their local times. And with those twenty-seven different times in Michigan, thirty-eight in Wisconsin, twenty-seven in Illinois, and twenty-three in Indiana, imagine the jumble. It drove the railroad people nuts.

Charles Dowd was a man who took this problem seriously. He wasn't even a railroad person; he was a teacher. His idea was to organize the United States into time zones so that everyone in each time zone would set their clocks and watches to the same time. He met with railroad officials, and he lectured to people whenever he could about the advantages of people giving up their own local times, to agree on a standard time.

Railroad Officials Untangle Time

Railroad officials were interested in Charles Dowd's ideas. They were pretty desperate by now. They had to straighten out the mess, and they knew that the only way to do this was to have some sort of uniform system. Officials from all the different railroad companies met in 1892 and formed an organization to deal with the situation.

William F. Allen was a member of that organization. He was a railroad engineer who had the same dream about time that Charles Dowd did. He also spent a lot of his time making a plan to untangle the mess.

Finally, on October 11, 1883, the railroad officials made a decision. They decided that all railroad clocks would be set according to four time zones in the United States. These were the eastern, central, mountain, and pacific time zones. The width of each time zone was made about equal to the distance that the sun seems to travel in one hour. On a map, lines of longitude run from the North Pole to the South Pole, all around the earth. Each time zone was fixed to cover 15 degrees of longitude.

The railroad officials decided that November 18, 1883, would be the day to reset all the clocks. That gave them over a month to get instructions to all railroad officials in the country, to notify town and city officials, and to inform newspapers so that everyone could learn about their solution.

This solution had two main results — it ended a big mess, and it started a big fuss. Even though lots of people across the country understood how this would simplify their lives, there were still people who could not be convinced. "The sun is supposed to rule the time, not the railroads," some argued. "This railroad time is contrary to nature," others argued. "You're robbing our daylight," still others said.

Some people thought that this was just a big plot cooked up by watchmakers so that lots of people would have to bring their watches in to be adjusted.

The Day of Two Noons

But even with the fuss, the solution went into effect as planned. November 18 was a Sunday, chosen because fewer trains ran on Sundays.

All the railroad stations in a time zone planned to set their clocks to noon at the same moment. The moment they decided on was when the sun would be at its peak in the center of the time zone. If you lived in the eastern part of a time zone, you had two noons on that Sunday. One was when noon usually came by the sun time where you lived. Another was when it was noon sun time in the center of your zone, and you reset your clocks.

If you lived in the western part of a time zone, you got to noon sooner than you would have. One newspaper said that you either lived a little of your life over again in the eastern parts of the time zones or were thrown into the future a little in the western sides. If you lived in Boston, the standard new noon came sixteen minutes after the usual noon. In the Chicago train station on that Sunday, the railroad officials stopped the station clock when it reached noon, and then they started it again after nine minutes and thirty-two seconds had passed. The new time was official.

In a town in Iowa, the fuss about the time change got to be a legal fuss. There was a fire right around the time when the fire insurance policy was supposed to expire. By the old sun time, the policy was in effect when the fire broke out. But by the new official time, the policy would have lapsed two and a half minutes before the fire broke out. The state Supreme Court said that the policy had been made when sun time was in effect and that it should be honored, so the insurance company had to pay.

Complaints continued, but pretty soon everyone got used to this new system. No one fussed any more, and the railroad people were happy.

Time Passes into Law

Even though everyone went along with the system that the railroad people set up, it wasn't really a legal system until thirty-five years later when Congress passed the Standard Time Act. That was on March 19, 1918. No one paid much attention to most of the law since they'd been using the four-zone time system for so long. But the law also set up a procedure so changes in the time zone boundaries could be made. Here's how the United States is divided into time zones.

You can see both the original 1883 zones and the ones that are used today. Notice that the boundary lines aren't very straight. They're kind of zigzaggy in places. This is so that nothing idiotic happens like a time zone change going right through your living room or through the middle of a town. Imagine what it would be like if your time was one hour different than your friend's time who lived a couple of blocks away? Think about some of the problems that would cause.

WHAT IF A TIME ZONE BOUNDARY WENT RIGHT THROUGH YOUR HOUSE ?

THE UNITED STATES DIVIDED INTO TIME ZONES

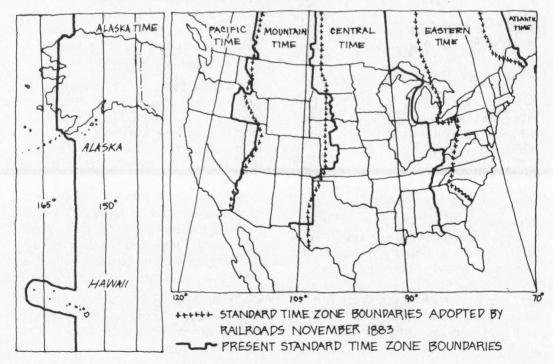

++++++ STANDARD TIME ZONE BOUNDARIES ADOPTED BY RAILROADS NOVEMBER 1883

PRESENT STANDARD TIME ZONE BOUNDARIES

After using the boundaries set by the railroads for a while, some kinks in the system were noticed. Towns that were near each other with lots of business going on between them were sometimes in two different time zones. The boundaries were changed. Sometimes a state didn't want to be chopped in two by a time zone, so these boundaries were changed too.

Which time zone do you live in? Can you figure out what time it is right now in New York or in Dallas or in Chicago or in Los Angeles?

Sun Noon and Clock Noon

When your clock says 12 noon, how close is that to when the sun is at its peak where you live? You can check this some sunny day when you're not in school. The easiest way is to have a friend stand straight and tall; then check his or her shadow. You need to check the shadow often until it seems to be as short as it's going to get. That's high noon according to the sun. Then check the clock time.

Here's another way. Get a piece of string a little longer than your arm and tie a rock to the end. A small rock will do, about as big around as a half-dollar. Next you need to find a place to tie the string so that the rock hangs down freely and you can see the shadow the rock and string make. A banister or railing outside will work, so will the low branch of a tree or a bush that lets the sunlight through enough. Or hang the string from a clothesline. You could poke a stick into the ground, but it has to be straight up and down. The rock at the end of the string will hang straight for sure. Whatever way you choose, check the shadow often, and when it gets to its shortest length, check the clock to see how close the time is to noon.

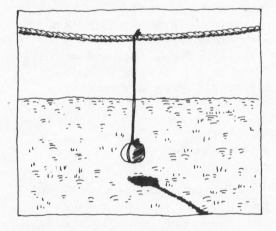

What you find will depend on several things. First of all, where you live in the time zone is important. If you're on the eastern edge of a time zone, the sun noon should be earlier than your clock says. The opposite will be true if you live on the western side of the time zone. Remember, the sun can't be directly overhead for everyone at the same time.

If it's daylight saving time when you try this experiment, your reading on the clock will be closer to 1:00 p.m. instead of noon. Keep on reading to learn about this time quirk.

Saving Daylight Time

In 1907, William Willett, an Englishman, published a pamphlet called "Waste of Daylight" in which he proposed daylight saving time. But the idea didn't catch on for almost ten years until it was first used in Germany in 1915. World War I was being fought then, and clocks were set ahead one hour to make more use of the daylight hours and so save energy. How do you think setting the clock ahead saves energy?

The law that Congress passed in 1917, the Standard Time Act, also included daylight saving time. Congress decided that everyone in the United States would go on daylight saving time permanently on March 30, 1918. But this ruling wasn't very popular with lots of people, so Congress changed that part of the law. Daylight saving time ended in October, 1919. But during World War II, Congress started it up again. The country was on daylight saving time from February 9, 1942, until after the war was over, September 30, 1945. Since that time, different communities decide whether or not to use daylight saving time.

Is daylight saving time used where you live? Most large northern cities use it; some smaller towns don't. The state of Arizona doesn't use daylight saving time, and it's not used in parts of Indiana. Farmers don't seem to like daylight saving time very much. They do all their work outside when the sun is up, and fiddling with the clocks is no help to them at all.

In places where daylight saving time is used, the clocks are changed on the last Sunday in April and October at 2 a.m. That's the official time for the change, but people don't get up in the middle of the night and stumble around the house resetting clocks. They either do it before they go to bed Saturday night or after they get up on Sunday.

Sunday was a smart day to pick. There are always some people who forget all about changing their clocks. If clocks were reset in the middle of the week, it's likely that some kids would get to school at the wrong time. They'd arrive an hour early or an hour late, depending on whether it was April or October.

Can you remember which way the clocks get moved? An old saying that helps is "Fall back, spring forward." This means that you set your clock back in the fall and ahead in the spring. Got that? Now if you totally forgot in April to reset your clock and went to school on Monday at the old time, would you be early or late?

TRY THIS QUIZ:

IF THIS WAS THE LAST SUNDAY IN APRIL, WOULD YOUR FRIEND BE EARLY, OR ARE YOU LATE? WHAT IF IT WAS THE LAST SUNDAY IN OCTOBER?

What About Moonlight Saving Time?

Do you think people will ever decide that it would be nice to have moonlight saving time for a change? What do you think that means, and how might it be done? Next time the moon is full, spend some time looking at how big and beautiful it is. Then give this idea some thought. You may come up with a good one.

The Rest of the World Clocks In

Not only the United States is divided into time zones; the entire world is. Time zones make life less confusing for everyone.

There are twenty-four time zones in all. This division was set up a year after the railroads organized time in the United States. An international time conference was held in October, 1884, in Washington, D. C. Representatives from twenty-six nations came and agreed to this twenty-four-zone system.

Take a look at Map One on the next page. It shows the general time zones in the northern half of the earth. The times noted are the hours of the day when it's noon in the central time zone in the United States. That's where Chicago is, so is St. Louis, New Orleans, Kansas City, and lots of other places. Look at the map and see if you can tell what time it is in Los Angeles? How about Paris? What about Peking? If it's noon in Chicago, what time is it where you live?

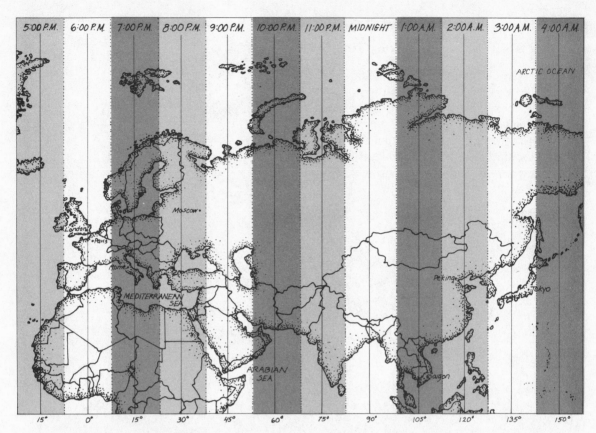

A Time Trip Around the Map

Map One

Take a time trip around the map and see how tricky the system really is. Use your index finger to do the traveling. Start on Map One by putting your finger right on Chicago, and think of it as being noon on Thursday. Now move over to Denver; it's Thursday at 11 a.m. Okay? And in San Francisco, it's Thursday at 10 a.m. Keep moving your finger in a westerly direction. In Fairbanks, it's 8 a.m. on Thursday. Go on to Peking. There it's 2 a.m., still Thursday. It's midnight on Thursday in Calcutta. But when you get to the next time zone, it's 11 p.m., which is the night before, Wednesday night. Follow the map around, moving your finger to the other side at Moscow. There it would be 8 p.m. on Wednesday. London and Paris would be 6 p.m., Wednesday. Back to the United States, and Philadelphia would be 1 p.m. on Wednesday.

You started this time zone trip around the map at noon on Thursday in Chicago. By reading the map correctly, you figured out that it was 1 p.m. in Philadelphia but on Wednesday. Now how can it be Thursday in Chicago and Wednesday in Philadelphia? Confused? Well, you ought to be. It's got to be the same day in all of the United States.

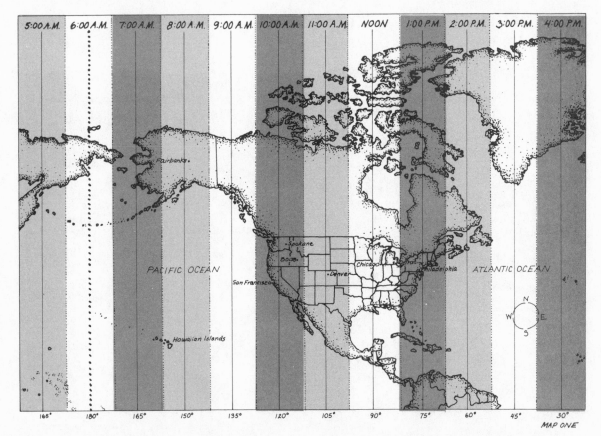

Sometimes Today Is Tomorrow

The problem of what day it is where was solved before it really became a problem. It was taken care of at the International Time Conference in 1884, at which they set up the International Date Line. That's the dotted line on the map west of Fairbanks, Alaska.

What happens is that when you're traveling west and you cross that line, the calendar moves ahead one day. When it's noon on Thursday in Chicago, and 10 a.m. on Thursday in San Francisco, and 8 a.m. in Fairbanks, still on Thursday, once you cross that dotted line, the day changes to Friday. So in Peking it's 2 a.m. on Friday. And when you get back to the time zone where it's 11 p.m., it's 11 p.m on Thursday. Follow that around the map. You should get back to Philadelphia this time on Thursday at 1 p.m. That puts Philadelphia and

Chicago on the same day, which is a relief. If you travel across the International Date Line the other way, from west to east, then you move back one calendar day.

The Real Time Zones

Take a look at Map Two. It's different from the other map. It shows the time zone lines as they really are. They're bent a lot to avoid chopping up places too much. Take the Hawaiian Islands, for example. In the first map, they're divided into two time zones. Not good. That's been taken care of in the second map. What other changes are there? Can you find places in the world where the sun time is still used? Why do you think the International Date Line was put in the middle of the Pacific Ocean and not down the middle of one of the continents?

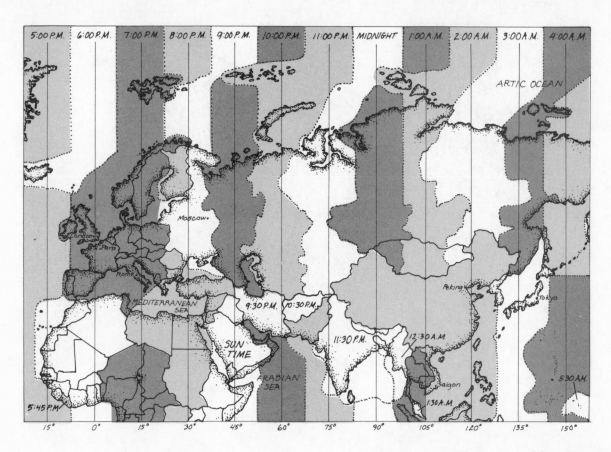

Map Two

A Time Tickler

Try this time riddle: Suppose someone you knew was living in Tokyo, Japan. Now suppose you wanted to call that person to wish them a Happy New Year so they'd get the call on December 31, just before midnight. At what time and what day would you have to place the call from where you live now?

Another Time Tickler

WHAT'S WRONG WITH THIS PICTURE?

NEW YORK   LONDON   ROME   PEKING   TOKYO

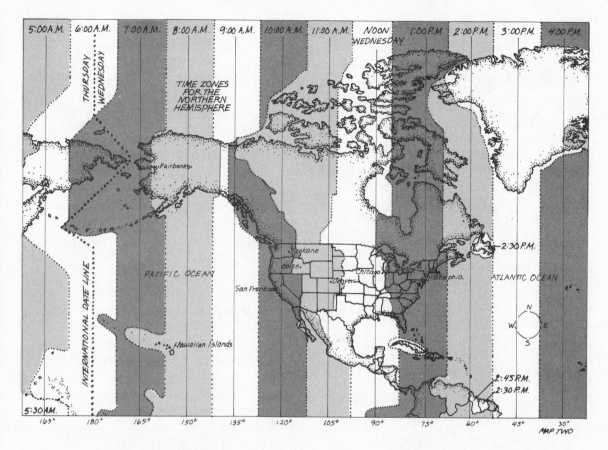

Time Zones for the Northern Hemisphere

MAP TWO

There Are Days When There Are No Nights

It's always a special treat in summertime to have the days so nice and long. There's plenty of time to play outside after eating supper. In winter, it gets dark pretty soon after you get home from school. You've probably noticed this for a long time, but have you thought about why this happens?

The reason for day and night is the spinning of the earth. You may have already learned about this in school. Imagine the earth as a ball with a knitting needle stuck through it. When you twirl the

knitting needle, the ball turns. Well, there's really nothing poked through the earth, but the earth spins as if there were. The earth has an imaginary line through it that's called the axis.

As the earth turns on its axis, it is day when the part of the earth where you live is facing the sun. It's night when where you live is away from the sun. The amount of time it takes for the earth to spin around once is what's measured by a twenty-four-hour day.

That's the reason for day and night, but this doesn't explain why days are longer in the summer and shorter in the winter. To understand that you have to put two more bits of information into the knitting-needle-and-ball explanation. One bit is that the imaginary knitting needle, the earth's axis, is not straight up and down. It's tipped on an angle that's figured to be just about 23½ degrees.

27

Here's a picture to help you see what that tip does. The top half of the earth that is tilted toward the sun will get more light over a larger area. In this drawing, the top half is where the United States is. That half of the earth is called the Northern Hemisphere. The other half is called the Southern Hemisphere.

Notice the part of the earth up at the top, near the axis. When the earth spins around, part of that top will always get some light from the sun. Can you imagine what it would be like to live that far north? It would be daylight when you went to bed, and it would be daylight when you got up. Nighttime would never get very dark at all.

Now imagine what it would be like to live way down at the tip of the Southern Hemisphere, where you would be in darkness all the time. Do you think you'd like that?

No part of the earth is in total daylight or darkness all the time. That's where the second bit of information comes in. This bit will help you understand why the lengths of day and night change. The earth does more than spin on its axis. It also rotates around the sun, making one complete round trip each year. On that trip around the sun, the same hemisphere is not always tilted toward the sun. See if this picture helps. Sometimes the northern tip is in darkness all day. Sometimes all parts of the earth seem to get some light and some dark every day.

The more sunlight the place you live gets during the year, the longer the days will be then. They will be warmer, too, which is why we have different seasons.

When you put all this information together, you'll understand how there can be days when there are no nights and also how there can be days when there is mostly darkness. Maybe someday you can visit one of those places during the right time of year and actually see what it is like to live in constant daytime or constant night.

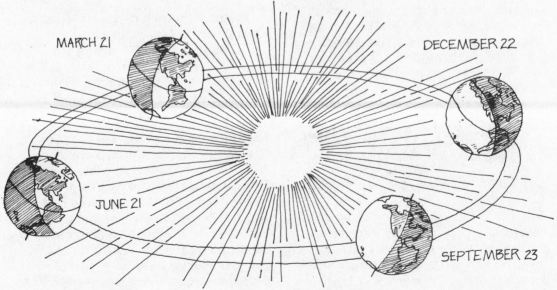

MARCH 21

DECEMBER 22

JUNE 21

SEPTEMBER 23

Chapter 3
Ticking Off the Day

Have you ever wondered why the day is divided into twenty-four hours? Try wondering about it right now. Why isn't the day divided into ten hours? The hours would be longer than they are now, but you could get used to that. (Can you figure how many of our minutes long each of those ten hours would be?) Or why not divide the day into fifty shorter hours? It might be a bit crowded on clock faces, but it would still be possible.

What's so special about twenty-four hours? Nothing, really. It's just that twenty-four hours have been used for so long that the idea stuck. It's a timely habit that everyone has gotten used to.

The Egyptians Start the Habit

The Egyptians were the first people known to divide the day into twenty-four hours. That was quite some time ago. But the ancient Egyptians did it differently than it is done today.

They took nighttime and divided that into twelve hours. Star watchers, who were priests, kept track of those hours by watching when particular stars appeared on the eastern horizon. Daytime, from sunrise to sunset, was divided into ten hours, and a shadow clock was used to keep track of those hours.

29

Then there were two more hours in the day, the twilight hours. One was dawn, just before the sun came up. The other was dusk, just after the sun went down. Those two, along with the ten daylight hours and the twelve nighttime hours, made up their twenty-four-hour day.

Every hour in this Egyptian system wasn't always the same length of time. In the summer, daylight lasts longer than it does in winter. So the Egyptian daytime hour was longer in the summer and shorter in the winter. Imagine how that would be if you took music lessons and had to practice an hour a day. How would that system affect TV schedules?

The Egyptian Shadow Clock

The Egyptian shadow clock was really a shadow watch. It was small and could be carried around easily. You can make one that is pretty much like the ones made before the eighth century B.C.

In the morning, the shadow clock needs to have the crossbar end to the east. Then in the afternoon, it needs to be turned around, with the crossbar end to the west.

Clocking by the Sun

The Egyptians weren't the only ones who used shadow clocks. It seems that whenever people wanted to make an instrument to keep time, they turned to the sun for help. This includes the ancient Chinese, the Babylonians, the ancient Greeks, and the Romans. Even after other kinds of clocks were invented, sundials were still used.

The idea of a shadow clock, or sundial, is simple. You need a post or stake stuck into the ground straight up and down. The word used for that post is *gnomon*. It comes from a Greek word meaning "one who knows." You follow the post's shadow as it moves during the day and mark off the hours. You can make one easily.

A Simple Sundial

Here's what you'll need: a pencil, half as long as a new one, about 4 inches; a small lump of clay; a piece of heavy paper or cardboard, around notebook size; a telephone book; some tape; a compass for finding north; a sunny day.

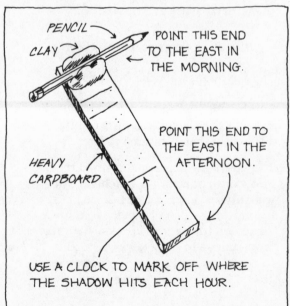

PENCIL
CLAY
POINT THIS END TO THE EAST IN THE MORNING.
HEAVY CARDBOARD
POINT THIS END TO THE EAST IN THE AFTERNOON.
USE A CLOCK TO MARK OFF WHERE THE SHADOW HITS EACH HOUR.

4" PENCIL
SMALL LUMP OF CLAY
HEAVY PAPER OR CARDBOARD
TELEPHONE BOOK
TELEPHONE DIRECTORY
TAPE
A COMPASS

Try to get started as early in the morning as you can after the sun comes up. Assemble this shadow clock outside, as the drawing shows. Make sure the pencil is as straight up and down as you can make it. Also make sure that you pick a level spot to set the sundial up.

Draw the shadow throughout the day, marking the hour at the tip of each shadow. Your pencil has to be short enough so that the end of the early morning shadow falls on the paper.

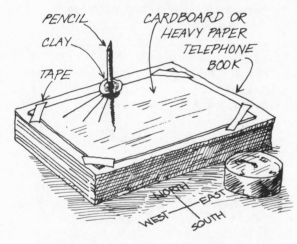

At the end of the day, connect the ends of the shadows with a line. The line should be curved. The shortest shadow of the day was when the sun was most directly overhead, but that may not have been when your clock said noon. Chapter 2 explains why this is so.

Your Clock Has Kinks

You can use your sundial the day after you make it to tell the time. But here's a kink. If you use it day after day for several months, you'll notice that the path of the shadow will change. It moves a tiny bit every day, even though it's hard to see this change until a large chunk of time has passed. The curve will be flattest in the summer and more curved in the winter.

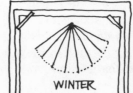

WINTER   SUMMER

You'll need a little patience to be able to see this for yourself. Write the date you made your shadow clock on it. Keep the clock in a safe place. When you notice another season has started, dig out your shadow clock. Then do the exact experiment again on the same paper, but use a pencil of another color to draw the shadows. Now compare the paths of the different shadows.

Another kink drove early sundial makers a little crazy. When you make the clock, you'll notice that the shadows you mark every hour aren't the same distances apart from each other. The shadow moves farther in an hour early and late in the day and not so far at midday. The clock wouldn't work very well if you marked off the hours evenly on the paper.

The Egyptians solved this problem by finding some way to figure these unequal distances, like on the shadow stick and on your shadow clock. But how did they know where to make the marks? Suppose you were making a sundial like this, and you didn't have a clock to mark off the hours. How could you make the correct marks?

Because of these kinks, people got interested in figuring out a way to make a sundial so that the hours would be evenly spaced on it, and it would work all through the year. A solution was found: Don't use a gnomon that is placed straight up and down after all; slant it, but at a special angle. To figure the angle took some fancy work, which kept those mathematicians and astronomers busy. The slant depends on where in the world the sundial will be used. Once, the Romans stole one of these sundials with a slanted gnomon from Egypt. When they got home, they were surprised to find that it didn't work.

You can make a fairly accurate sundial with a slanting gnomon at home. If you haven't learned about measuring angles yet, you may need some help from an older brother or sister or one of your parents.

Sundial Number Two

COLLECT THE SUPPLIES YOU'LL NEED:

- A SQUARE PIECE OF HEAVY CARD-BOARD, ABOUT TWELVE INCHES ON A SIDE

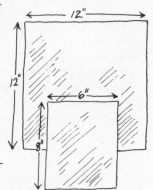

- ANOTHER PIECE OF HEAVY CARDBOARD, ABOUT SIX INCHES BY EIGHT INCHES

- A MAP SHOWING WHERE YOU LIVE AND THE LATITUDE LINES

- A PROTRACTOR FOR MEASURING THE ANGLE OF YOUR GNOMON

- SOME TAPE

- A COMPASS FOR FINDING NORTH

- A TELEPHONE BOOK

- A PAIR OF SCISSORS

FOLLOW THESE DIRECTIONS.

1. ON A MAP, LOOK UP THE LATITUDE WHERE YOU LIVE.

2. ON THE SMALLER PIECE OF CARDBOARD, DRAW A DOTTED BASE LINE AS SHOWN.

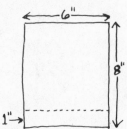

3. MEASURE YOUR ANGLE OF LATITUDE FROM THE BASE LINE AND DRAW THE ANGLE LINE.

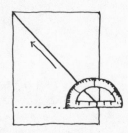

4. CUT ALONG THIS LINE TO MAKE THE GNOMON.

5. BEND THE GNOMON ALONG THE DOTTED LINE. SCORING IT FIRST WITH THE TIP OF THE SCISSORS HELPS.

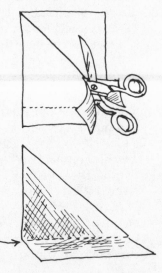

6. TAPE THE GNOMON TO THE LARGER PIECE OF CARDBOARD, CLOSE TO THE CENTER OF ONE EDGE.

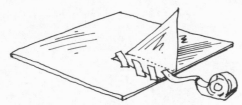

7. THE GNOMON NEEDS TO BE UPRIGHT. CUT A SMALL TRIANGLE FROM THE EXTRA CARDBOARD. FOLD IT AND TAPE AS SHOWN

8. TAPE THE BASE TO A TELEPHONE BOOK.

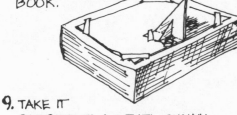

9. TAKE IT OUTSIDE TO A LEVEL, SUNNY SPOT. USE A COMPASS TO FIND NORTH AND FACE YOUR SUNDIAL AS SHOWN.

10. NOW YOU'RE READY TO MARK THE HOURS ON THE DIAL. START EARLY IN THE DAY AND CHECK A CLOCK EACH HOUR. MARK OFF THE SPOTS ON THE EDGES OF THE CARDBOARD.

An eight-hundred-page book was published in the year 1612 to help sundial makers figure how to mark off the dial accurately. Lucky for you, you can use a clock to do this work.

There still are kinks with this type of sundial. It wouldn't be much help for timing a three-minute boiled egg, for example. That didn't bother people long ago, but just don't expect too much from your sundial today.

There's even a bigger kink. There's no way at all to tell the time when the sun isn't shining.

Noon with a Boom

An ingenious sundial was made in England in the mid-1600s. It not only marked the hours, but it shot a cannon every day at noon. There was a small cannon on the flat dial. A magnifying glass was fixed so that when the sun was at its highest point, its rays would be focused on a gunpowder fuse. The sun and magnifying glass would cause the fuse to light and set off the cannon. Noon was pretty noisy on sunny days.

A Clock That Drips

There was still another kink in the sundial method of timekeeping. It wasn't ever any use at night. One solution to this was found by Prince Amenemhet.

The Prince lived in ancient Egypt. The king at that time, Amenophis I, was interested in finding a way to tell the time during the night without having to crawl out of bed and figure out which stars were where. Besides, on a cloudy night, that was no better than a shadow clock on a cloudy day. So Prince Amenemhet made a water clock for the king.

This clock took the shape of a big bucket. At nightfall, it was filled with water up to a marked line. There was a small hole near the bottom of the bucket, and the water trickled out slowly. Inside the bucket, lines were marked that showed the hours. All the king had to do was light a torch and take a peek in the bucket to count how many lines he could see. Or he could just estimate by sticking his hand in and feeling how far down the water level was. That was definitely more convenient than going outside into the cold night to squint at the stars through sleepy eyes.

Does it seem like a simple idea? You can make one to try. (You can try yours in the daytime.) This is a simple version of Prince Amenemhet's attempt.

Water Clock Number One

THIS CLOCK IS FOR SHORT TIME PERIODS. HERE'S WHAT YOU NEED:
- A STYROFOAM CUP OR SMALL EMPTY YOGURT CONTAINER
- A SMALL GLASS JAR
- A STRIP OF PAPER
- TWO RUBBER BANDS
- A PIN

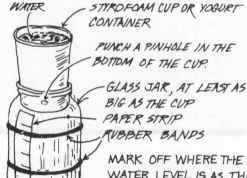

WATER

STYROFOAM CUP OR YOGURT CONTAINER

PUNCH A PINHOLE IN THE BOTTOM OF THE CUP.

GLASS JAR, AT LEAST AS BIG AS THE CUP
PAPER STRIP
RUBBER BANDS

MARK OFF WHERE THE WATER LEVEL IS AS THE WATER DRIPS INTO THE JAR. DO THIS AT FIVE—MINUTE INTERVALS. SETTING A KITCHEN TIMER HELPS, IF YOU HAVE ONE, TO REMIND YOU. WHEN YOU MARK THE TIME, THE MARKS ON THE PAPER SCALE WILL BE FARTHER APART AS YOU GET UP HIGHER. WHY DO YOU THINK THIS IS SO?

Prince Amenemhet had some problems with his clock. During the night, the temperature goes down, and water flows more slowly when it is cooler. After you've got your water clock made and the time marked off, try using ice water and see if that affects your timekeeping. It's a hard problem, and Prince Amenemhet never did figure a way to solve it.

What do you think soapy water would do to your water clock? Squeeze a little squirt of liquid soap into the cup and try it.

Legal Dripping

Another name for a water clock is *clepsydra*. This word comes from two Greek words that mean "thief" and "water." Clepsydras were used in legal courts during Greek and Roman times. They were used to time speeches given by lawyers. One officer of the court was in charge of watching the clepsydra and announcing when a speaker's time was up. Sometimes, though, a lawyer with a lot to say would bribe the officer to put some mud in the water to keep it from flowing so quickly.

Clepsydras Get Complicated

People began to invent other ways to use the waterpower of this clock. Here's one example. A float rises as the container fills up. It pushes a notched rod

---

Water Clock Number Two

IF YOU'RE IN THE MOOD FOR A FANCIER VERSION, TRY PUTTING TOGETHER A CLOCK LIKE THIS. IT'S DESIGNED AFTER A CHINESE INVENTION. FIRST, COLLECT THE SUPPLIES YOU'LL NEED:
- FIVE STYROFOAM CUPS OR EMPTY YOGURT CONTAINERS
- ONE SMALL GLASS JAR, AT LEAST AS BIG AS EACH OF THE CUPS
- TWO RUBBER BANDS
- A PIN
- A STRIP OF PAPER
- FOUR THUMBTACKS

HERE'S HOW TO ASSEMBLE THIS CLOCK. ASK PERMISSION TO TACK THE CUPS INTO THE WALL SOMEWHERE OR USE A STRIP OF WOOD OR HEAVY CARDBOARD, IF YOUR PARENTS OBJECT TO GETTING HOLES POKED INTO THE WALLS.

HOW LONG DO YOU THINK IT WILL TAKE TO FILL THE GLASS JAR WITH THIS CLOCK?

FILL UP THE TOP CUP.

PUNCH A PIN HOLE IN EACH CUP.

MARK OFF THE PAPER SCALE IN FIVE-MINUTE INTERVALS.

up that turns a gear that turns the pointer that points to the hour on a dial. This device looks more like a modern clock than any of the earlier timekeepers. Check out the funnel that feeds in the water. It's kept continually full, with the excess water dripping out. That way, the water flows into the bottom container with the same pressure all the time. This keeps the gear turning regularly. Do you think you could build one like this?

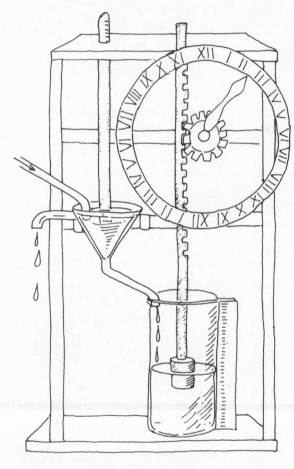

Water clocks weren't ideal. When it got very cold out, the water would freeze. When it got very hot, the water would evaporate too quickly. If the water got dirty, it would be slowed down. But even so, they were widely used in many countries.

The Incredible Clepsydra

Have you ever read the Arabian stories, *A Thousand and One Nights?* Harun-al-Raschid is a hero in those stories. He gave a clepsydra to Emperor Charlemagne in 807 to impress him with the wealth of Baghdad. This is a true story. It was made of brass and inlaid gold. It had a dial, and each hour on the dial was marked with a tiny door. When 1 o'clock came, the first door opened, and a small metal ball rolled out and hit a brass bell. At 2 o'clock, the next door opened, and two small balls dropped out and chimed the hours on the bell. This kept on until 12 o'clock. At both noon and midnight, a golden horseman appeared in each door and shut them all to start the sequence again. And all this was run by water.

From Wet to Dry

Sand clocks ended those water problems. Sand didn't freeze. Hot weather didn't bother sand. The clocks were sealed so no pebbles or dirt could get in and obstruct the sand's flow. Also a sand clock could be carried easily without the problem of sloshing water.

No one knows for sure who first thought of sand clocks, but they were used a lot up to the middle of the seventeenth century, and they're still used today. Some people have egg timers around that are tiny sand clocks. Is there one in your house?

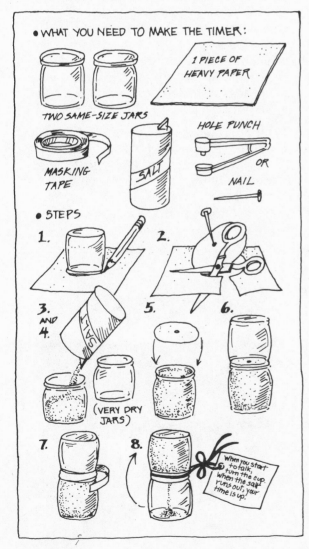

● WHAT YOU NEED TO MAKE THE TIMER:

1 PIECE OF HEAVY PAPER

TWO SAME-SIZE JARS

MASKING TAPE

SALT

HOLE PUNCH

OR

NAIL

● STEPS

1.

2.

3. AND 4.

(VERY DRY JARS)

5.

6.

7.

8.

When you start to talk, turn the cup, when the salt runs out, your time is up!

Is there someone in your house who likes soft-boiled eggs cooked just so? Or do you need a telephone timer to keep track of who's hogging the phone? Why not make a timer yourself? Here's how.

You need: two jars that are the same size, a piece of heavy paper, masking tape, salt, a hole punch or a nail.

Follow these directions.

1. Trace a circle the size of the mouth of the jars on the heavy paper. Cut it out.

2. Punch a hole in the center of this circle. A hole punch makes a nice clean hole with no rough edges. Use a nail if you don't have a punch.

3. Make sure the jars are absolutely dry. Putting them in a warm oven (150 degrees Fahrenheit) for half an hour should do it.

4. Pour salt into one jar almost to the top.

5. Put the paper circle over the mouth of this jar.

6. Place the mouth of the other jar carefully on top of the circle.

7. With the two jars lined up carefully, tape them together so they're well sealed.

That's it. Turn the timer upside-down, and time how long it takes the salt to run through to the other jar. It will take some fiddling to get the timer adjusted to the exact time you want. You may have to take it apart several times to do this. You've got two choices: you can make the hole larger or smaller, or you can adjust the amount of salt you use.

When you've got it right, tie a string around the place the jars are joined and attach a cheery tag: *Egg timer specially designed to cook your eggs just how you like them.* Or *When you start to talk, turn the cup, when the salt runs out, your time is up.*

The First Tick

Finally a clock was invented that didn't drip or run dry or depend on the sun or need a supply of sand. This one actually ticked. It was a mechanical clock, and the early ones were built by the beginning of the fourteenth century.

No one is positively sure who the inventor was. But they're pretty sure that the biggest efforts to get this clock invented were made by mechanically minded monks, who wanted to be sure to call people to prayer at the right times.

These first mechanical clocks used a slowly dropping weight to move the gears that moved the pointer that showed the hour. They were built in tall towers, since the weights needed a good distance to fall.

Some people thought that these clocks were pretty remarkable. Some suspected, though, that there was a trick, that the clocks didn't really work by themselves at all, and that someone was hiding in the tower moving the works. But all people marveled at what good time these clocks kept. They were hardly ever off more than two hours in a day! That really wasn't much better than the water clocks. And it's not a very good tick record by today's standards.

There are still some of these clocks around. Maybe someday you can go see them for yourself. The big clock at Rouen in Normandy, France, was built in 1389. It was there when Joan of Arc was on trial. And it's still working today, even though its parts have had to be changed. There's another one in Salisbury, England, that you can see. This one is believed to be the oldest still existing, made in 1386.

There are some modern versions of these weight-driven clocks still being built. Have you ever seen a cuckoo clock? They usually run by weights. If you know someone who has one or if you're in a store where they are sold, ask about them.

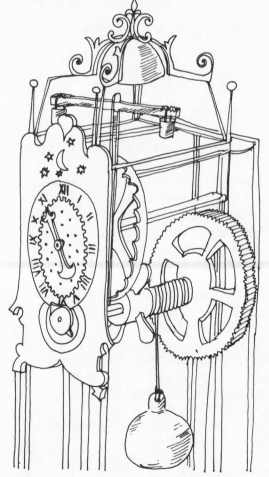

Show Time

These early mechanical clocks often put on a good show. Some of them did lots more than move a pointer around a dial. Some had knights on horseback that would come out and joust on the hour. Other clocks had chariots that came out, pulled by mechanical oxen. Ferocious-looking animals appeared each hour on some clocks. Sometimes there were figures that came out and banged out the hours on bells with mallets. One had a mechanical rooster that appeared and flapped its wings and crowed every day at noon. The citizens of the town during these medieval times seemed to like the clock shows a lot. Maybe that's why they didn't care if they didn't keep such terrific time.

The Swing to Better Time

The big breakthrough in clockmaking came about because of a discovery by Galileo Galilei. He lived in Italy in the sixteenth century. The story goes that when he was seventeen years old, in 1581, he noticed a very curious thing. He noticed this curious thing while he was standing in the Cathedral of Pisa.

His mind wasn't on religion for sure. It was occupied watching the enormous chandelier hanging from the dome swing back and forth because of a draft from the church door opening and closing. What was so interesting to Galileo was that no matter whether the chandelier made a wide arc or a short arc, it seemed to take the same time to move from one end of its arc to the other. He checked this observation by timing the swings against his pulse.

The chandelier was like a big pendulum, and if it really took the same time to move back and forth in each swing, maybe such a device could be used to keep a clock ticking in time. Galileo spent lots more time investigating pendulums during his life.

Getting in the Swing

You can try some of the experiments that Galileo did to learn about how pendulums behave. Pendulums have pretty amazing habits, and they're easy to investigate. You'll need some equipment:

- A BALL OF STRING

- FOUR WEIGHTS, TWO THAT ARE THE SAME, AND TWO OTHER ONES THAT ARE DIFFERENT. (YOU CAN USE LUMPS OF CLAY, TENNIS OR OTHER BALLS, FISHING WEIGHTS, A SET OF KEYS FROM ONE OF YOUR PARENTS, ROCKS, ANY SMALL TOYS.)

- A WATCH WITH A SECOND HAND

- A DOORWAY

- FOUR CUP HOOKS OR EYE HOOKS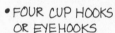

Set up your experiment by screwing in the cup or eyehooks in a doorway. Be sure to get permission from your parents first, because they will make holes. You can do it outside if you can find a place where a pendulum can swing freely.

Tie one of your weights to a length of string so it hangs as shown.

Now you can try to see what Galileo noticed in the cathedral. It is good to have a friend help when you're doing these experiments. Then one of you can do the timing while the other counts the swings of the pendulum.

Start the pendulum by holding the weight out and letting it go. Say "Go" when you release it so your friend can start timing. After you count ten one-way swings, say "Stop." How long did that take?

Try the experiment again, but this time don't start the pendulum so far out. Time ten more swings and see how long they take this time. According to Galileo's observation, both trials should take the same amount of time, even though the size of the swing is different.

Don't stop here. There's lots more you can learn about. Try these experiments.

1. Change the weight at the end of the swing. Do you think this will affect how much time it takes for the pendulum to make ten swings? Try it.

2. Change the length of the string and try the experiment again. What happens this time?

40

were bowling pins. Give one pendulum a swing and see how many tees the pendulum knocks down before it stops. Keep score.

You can change the rules as you like. Try playing by swinging two pendulums at once. Allow two tries instead of one to knock them down. Use twenty-five tees, arranged in a five by five square. Try it with eight tees in a straight line across the doorway entrance. How good you get at these games depends on how much you figure out about the way pendulums really swing.

3. Hook up another pendulum. Try to get the two of them to swing together for ten swings. Try for twenty swings. And try it with different weights on the end of each string, and see if that affects their swinging together.

4. Can you hook up a pendulum so it makes ten swings in just about ten seconds?

Which do you think would be the main factor in changing the timing of the swings of the pendulum: the length of the string, how heavy the weight is, or both? Try the experiments now to find out for yourself.

Pendulum Bowling

You might want to try some pendulum games once you've got all this set up. You'll need some wooden golf tees or short pegs to play these. Use weights that are no bigger around than a golf ball.

Fix the pendulums so they hang low enough to knock over a golf tee if they hit it during a swing. Take turns with your friend. Set up the tees as if they

41

A Contraction in Time

O'clock is just a short-cut way of saying "of the clock." It's the same kind of short cut that lots of people's names have taken, like O'Neill or O'Reilly. Those names first meant "of the Neill family" or "of the Reilly family."

The Colossal Clock Contest

Imagine this. Suppose you are on a ship at sea. All you can see in every direction is water. You have a map that is marked off in latitude and longitude lines, but there are no signposts or clues out there in the middle of the ocean to give you a hint about your position.

This is the problem that all sailors faced for centuries. They solved one part of the problem very early. That's the latitude part. *Latitude* is the word that describes distances north and south of the equator. If you look at a map or globe, you'll see the lines of latitude running east and west. They're all parallel to each other, and sometimes they're called parallels. Sailors learned long ago how to use Polaris, the polestar, to figure out their latitude at sea, so they knew how far north or south they were.

But longitude was trickier. Longitude tells you how far east or west you are. If you don't know, you risk bumping into something unexpected — like some islands you can't see because it is nighttime or very foggy. That's exactly what happened to Sir Cloudsley Shovel. He was admiral of the British fleet. In 1707, which was before anyone had an accurate way to figure longitude at sea, poor Sir Cloudsley's fleet crashed into the Scilly Islands. Four ships and two thousand sailors were lost, including Sir Cloudsley.

The British government had had enough of this. They decided it was time to solve the longitude problem once and for all. In 1714, they announced a contest. Whoever built a clock that would keep accurate time out at sea would get a prize of twenty thousand British pounds. That's lots more than twenty thousand United States dollars today.

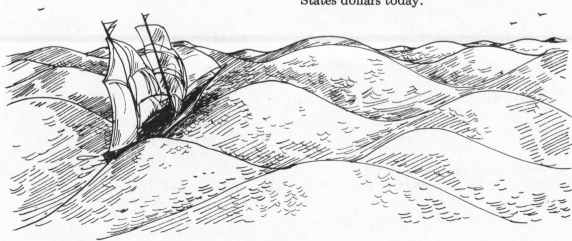

Why a clock? What does a clock have to do with longitude? Imagine yourself back at sea again. You've got a map that shows the longitude lines like the time zone map on pages 24 and 25 does. The time zone boundaries all run north and south, just like the lines of longitude. You've also got your trusty wristwatch that you set to the correct time when you set sail from New York.

So there you are, sailing along somewhere in the Atlantic Ocean. You can tell from the sun that it's just about high noon where you now are, but you've kept track on your watch, so you know it's only 8:00 in the morning back in New York. That's four hours earlier. Check the map on pages 26 and 27. If it's 8:00 a.m. in New York, count over four time zones to the east to see where in the Atlantic it is noon now. That gives you your approximate position. That's how a clock could help.

There were no trusty wristwatches back then, however, and even though great improvements had been made in clocks before this, they weren't accurate enough to do the job at sea. A clock was needed that would be accurate to a fraction of a second a day.

Lots of people got busy when the contest was announced. The prize was a lot of money. But it was almost fifty years before anyone solved the problem.

John Harrison Gets to Work

The person who finally did it was John Harrison. He was a carpenter, but he loved to tinker with timepieces. It was his hobby. He often fixed friends' clocks, and he had even built an entire grandfather clock by himself. In 1728, John Harrison was thirty-five years old. He heard about the contest that had been announced fourteen years before. Since no one had found a solution yet, he decided to try.

Six years after he started working on the problem, John Harrison had a clock that he thought would work. It was a monster of a clock. It weighed seventy-two pounds and was two feet long and a foot and a half wide. It looked like a weird piece of machinery invented by some mad scientist. It was tested in 1734, and though it was promising, it still wasn't accurate enough.

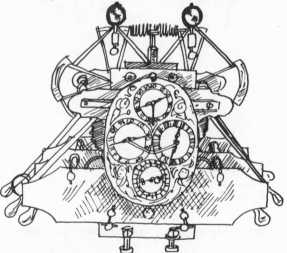

So John Harrison went back to work on another clock. This one took him three years to build. It was even bigger and heavier than the first clock. It weighed 103 pounds. When it was ready, in 1739, England was at war with Spain. All the ships were busy at battle, and there were no spare ships to be sailing around testing another monster clock.

But John Harrison wasn't discouraged. (Can you imagine not being discouraged after nine years of work with no success? He was a determined man.) The third clock took him seventeen years to build! He was very sure that this one would work, but while he was building it, he had an idea for an even better one. So he started building number four without even testing the third one. The fourth took him two years to make. It was much, much smaller, about the size of an alarm clock. It ran for thirty days without rewinding, and it was beautifully made.

The Clock Goes to Sea

In 1761, this fourth clock was finally tested. John Harrison was sixty-eight years old then and too old to make a long voyage. So his son William took the clock on board the British ship, H.M.S. Deptford. It sailed from England, headed for Jamaica, across the Atlantic Ocean.

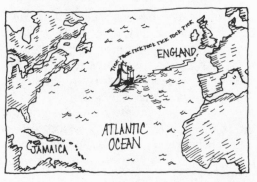

The first scheduled stop of the trip was the island of Madeira. After nine days at sea, William predicted their longitudinal position using the clock his father had built. "If you keep on this course, you'll be able to see land tomorrow," he told Captain Digges.

Captain Digges didn't believe him. "I've sailed these seas often, lad, and if I follow what you say, we'll never see Madeira."

It was important to the captain and the whole crew to reach Madeira. There was no more beer on board, and that was where they picked up a fresh supply. But since it was also important to test the clock, he agreed to do what William suggested.

At 6:00 the next morning, William was already awake when he heard the cry, "Land ho-o-o!" That was a happy moment for William, though his dad didn't hear about it for a while. The trip to Jamaica took 161 days. When they arrived there, the clock was only off by five seconds.

When William got back to England, his father was joyous. Can you possibly imagine what it would be like to work on something that was very, very important to you for as long as John Harrison did — over thirty years — and finally have it work perfectly? Collecting the prize money didn't work as well, however. This was another struggle that took

John ten more years and the help of George III, the king of England at that time. The committee members who were in control of the money just weren't sure they wanted to part with it. But finally, at the age of seventy-nine, John Harrison collected all that he deserved and got to enjoy it for four more years until he died at the age of eighty-three.

The type of clock used today aboard ships isn't the same design as the one John Harrison invented. Other inventors worked on the same problem. Today, the timekeeper used on ships is called a chronometer. Even though it isn't built like John Harrison's number four, there's no doubt that his was the first to actually work.

More Exact Clocking

Back on land, for two hundred years, pendulum clocks were still the most accurate clocks used. They were continually improved. By 1900, pendulum clocks were made that were off no more than 1/100 of a second a day. That's probably good enough for any timekeeping needs most people have. But clocks have been invented that do even better.

In the 1920s, scientists found that they could keep better time using quartz crystals rather than a pendulum. The quartz crystal clocks can keep time to within 2/1000 of a second each year.

In 1956, clocks were built that kept even better time than that — the atomic clocks. These are not household clocks. They're big and expensive. But they're so accurate that they can keep time to an accuracy of 3/100,000 of a second a year. That means an atomic clock won't be off more than one second every thirty thousand years. There's more about these incredible clocks in Chapter 5.

The Twenty-Four-Hour Clock

How come there are only twelve hours marked on clocks and watches when there are twenty-four hours in the day? Why don't the hours get numbered past twelve? Then there wouldn't be any need for a.m. or p.m. to make sure that the time is correctly understood.

That's another of those time habits that started a long time ago and stuck. But a twenty-four-hour system is used in some countries to say the time, even with twelve-hour clock faces. The military uses it too. Here's how this system works.

The hours are numbered from 0:00 to 23:59. Midnight is zero hour. After 12 noon, which is 12:00, comes 13:00. It's said in hundreds, like thirteen hundred. By this system, you get out of school around fifteen hundred. And you eat dinner around eighteen hundred. How would you say the time that you usually go to bed on school nights according to this system?

Clock Riddles

These are pretty tricky. Lewis Carroll thought of them. He was a mathematician and the person who wrote *Alice in Wonderland*. He had a terrific imagination. He wrote these riddles in the late 1800s, before anyone had thought of quartz crystal clocks or atomic clocks. See what you think about his riddles.

Riddle Number One: Which keeps better time, a clock that is right once every two years or a clock that is right twice every day?

Well, what do you think? Most people pick the right-twice-a-day clock as the better choice. Did you? Read on.

Riddle Number Two: Which clock works better, one that loses a minute a day or one that doesn't run at all?

Now what do you think? The lose-a-minute-a-day seems like the better choice to most people.

Here's where the tricky part comes in. Lewis Carroll figured that the clock that loses a minute a day will take a long time before it ever hits the right time again. Just about two years, because it won't be right again until it loses twelve hours, which is 720 minutes, which is just about two years at a minute lost a day. So it will only be right once every two years.

But suppose the clock that doesn't run is stuck at 8:00. It will be correct twice a day, when the time really does roll around to 8:00 in the morning and 8:00 at night. Check back to Riddle Number One. Which do you think is the better answer now?

A Clockless World

Suppose that for one day, all the clocks in the world broke down. There wasn't one that worked; not even the telephone time service was operating. How would that change your life? How would that change things in the world? If you're the kind of person who likes to write stories or poems, it might be fun to try a story or poem called "A Clockless World."

Chapter 4
Portable Time

The search for time that people could carry around with them started back in the 1500s. That was before pendulum clocks were invented and before any clocks kept very good time at all. Those first small clocks invented then didn't do very well either in their timekeeping. But the idea of portable time caught on, and portable timepieces have gotten better and better since then.

Jewelry That Ticked

Peter Heinlein was the first to figure out how to build a clock small enough to carry around. This was in the early 1500s. At that time, most clocks were the big tower clocks, run by slowly dropping weights on long ropes. That idea would never do for watches.

But Peter Heinlein, a locksmith in Nuremberg, Germany, had an idea. His invention was a coiled spring that you wound up. The spring provided the power to keep the watch ticking. It worked. It did keep the watch ticking, but not well enough to keep very accurate time.

The problem was that right after you wound it up, the spring was real tight and moved the hour hand right along. When it unwound a bit though, the spring lost power, and the hour hand slowed down. There wasn't any minute hand to worry about. It wouldn't have been any help anyway. The hour hand was usually off anywhere from half an hour to two hours each day.

These watches weren't very small compared to today's watches. They were about the size and shape of goose eggs. Because of this, they came to be called Nuremberg eggs.

A WATCH FROM THE EARLY 1600S

Rich people, who lived in Europe and had lots of extra money to spend, loved watches. They wore them on chains around their necks or hanging from their belts. Watches were a big fad, not for keeping time as much as for how they looked. They were often made from gold or silver. They were beautifully engraved, with jewels embedded in them. And they were made in lots of different shapes — to look like animals or shells or flowers. Sometimes they were built right into the knobs of canes.

Pocket Time Improves

When the pendulum clock was invented, it didn't help the pocket-watch problem at all. Pendulums were no use in watches. They would get all out of whack being jostled in a pocket or swinging from your neck or belt.

The hairspring was invented in 1665. A hairspring is a vibrating spring. It has a regular rhythm and keeps even time. This invention gave the small timepieces a big boost. It solved the problem of the coiled spring keeping such uneven time. Over the years, lots more improvements have been made. Glass covers were added to protect the hands. Since the watches were so much more accurate, minute hands were added. Second hands too. Jewels were added around 1700 to help watches run more smoothly. The jewels eliminated the friction points in the works of the watch. Automatic winding was invented around 1770.

Skull Time

Mary, Queen of Scots, had a watch made that was shaped like a skull. It was made from silver. To tell the time, you had to hold it upside-down and open the hinged jaw. The dial was in the part of the skull where the brain would be.

Jewels in Your Watch

If you've got a watch that has seventeen jewels, that means that seventeen friction points are eased by tiny jewels. Tiny chips of real sapphires and rubies used to be used, but most of these "jewels" are synthetic today.

Why Are They Called Watches?

Once the hairspring was invented, the pocket timepieces became very useful on board ships. Before then, the pendulum clocks had not been very useful. If a pendulum got bumped about in your pocket, imagine what would happen at sea. Not even the most dedicated pendulum could swing regularly on a rolling ship.

On board ship, there are times during the day and night when different sailors are on duty. This duty is called standing watch. The pocket clocks, made with hairsprings, were used to time the length of the watches. They've been called watches ever since.

Watches Move to Wrists

It was a long time before people thought to wear their watches on their wrists. When watches were first made, they were much too big and heavy for a person to drag around on their hand all day. And when they were made smaller, the wrist idea just didn't catch on.

There were some watchmakers who made very small watches in the eighteenth and nineteenth centuries. But they went just too far. They made watches small enough for rings and earrings, but they couldn't get them to keep very good time. Besides how would you tell the time if your watch was hanging from your ear?

In 1880, the Imperial German Navy decided that its officers ought to have their watches strapped to their wrists. Officers had enough to do to keep their balance on rolling ships when the decks were wet and slippery without having to dig around in their pockets for the right time.

Slowly, people realized how convenient this was. By the early 1900s, wearing wristwatches became popular for almost everyone.

Watches with the faces of popular characters were created, and Mickey Mouse became a big timekeeper in 1934. That's when he first appeared on wristwatches with his arms pointing to the time. These watches became an instant hit and a fad much more widespread than the Nuremberg eggs. Millions of Mickey Mouse watches have been made, and people all over the world have worn them. The manufacturers stopped making them in 1960, but since then they have started up again. What other cartoon characters have you seen on watches?

A Watch with Extras

In 1900, a watch was made by a French company and put on display at the Paris Exposition that year. It was a fantastically complicated timekeeper. Here's what this watch told you: the day, date, and year for the whole twentieth century, the phases of the moon, the seasons, solstices, and equinoxes, the positions of the heavens for the Northern Hemisphere, the positions of the heavens for the Southern Hemisphere, and the daily sunrise and sunset time in Lisbon. This watch chimed every quarter-hour. It could work as a stopwatch. It had a thermometer built in, as well as a barometer, an altimeter, and a compass. And it told the time in hours and minutes for 125 cities in the world. It took three years to make and weighed one pound. Somehow it never caught on. Can you imagine why?

Is There a Watch in Your Life?

Do you own your own watch? If you do, can you remember how old you were when you got it, and if it was a special present? For many kids, getting a watch is a very special thing. It's something that happens when the grownups in your life think you're ready for it somehow. What do you think makes you ready?

Take a survey of your friends and see how watches fit into their lives. Ask them these four questions, and keep a tally of their answers.

1. Do you think wearing a watch is important?

2. Do you have a watch?

(Skip these next two if the answer to Number 2 was no.)

3. How old were you when you got your first watch?

4. Does your watch have hands or is it a digital watch?

What do you think most of your friends would answer to these questions? Make your predictions first, and then see if your predictions hold true.

What about grownups? Do you think most of them wear watches? Check around and see. You might try the same four questions with them to see how grownups' answers compare with kids' answers.

Does Your Watch Tick or Hum?

There is a watch made that doesn't tick. It hums, and you can hear the faint hum if you hold it to your ear. The Bulova Accutron was the first one like this. It was made in 1960.

A miniature tuning fork is what keeps the time. Have you ever seen a tuning fork? It looks like the letter U on a stick, and when you strike it against a hard surface, it vibrates and produces a hum. In the tuning-fork watch, the pulses of electricity from the power cell in the watch keep the tuning fork inside vibrating. And it hums a steady note just between E and F above middle C. It keeps very accurate time.

Up-to-Date Wrist Time

Digital electronic watches are the biggest watch news of the century. The first one was built in 1952. These watches keep time in a way Peter Heinlein never imagined when he was tinkering with his Nuremberg eggs.

Most of the digital watches have what's called a four-digit read-out. That's so there's space for all the possible times from 1:00 to 12:59. How can all those different numbers be possible in a small amount of space? Most watches use what's called a seven-segment read-out system. A pattern like this is made from seven line segments:

Depending on which parts of this pattern light up, any of the digits from 0 to 9 can be made,

like 5 or 3 or 1

Make some little sketches to show yourself how all the digits are possible.

This same seven-segment display can make some of the letters of the alphabet, like E, F, H, J, L, P, O, U, C, I, h, b, d. Could you spell your name with this system? Or could you spell some words, like HELLO ?

Some of these watches tell the date too. Others have dots that light up to show whether it's a.m. or p.m. Most of them don't show the time all day long. You have to push a button to see it. That's to conserve power and not run the battery down so fast.

The batteries in these watches usually run for one year before needing to be replaced. They will wear out faster if you look at your watch lots more times than the watch manufacturers count on. They figure that people look at their watches about twenty-five times a day, and that's what they've used to estimate the one-year life of the battery.

Digital electronic watches keep very precise time. They're off no more than three minutes a year. Can you think of any reason why you'd need a watch more accurate than that?

GOT A SECOND?

NET WEIGHT: ONE MINUTE

CONTENTS: SIXTY INDIVIDUAL SECONDS

ABOUT 5"?

Chapter 5
Bits of Time

Does a second seem like a short amount of time to you? A very short amount of time? Do you know what a second feels like?

Try this experiment. You need a watch or clock with a second hand. See if you can estimate how long ten seconds is without looking at the watch or clock. The easiest way to try would be with a friend. Then your friend could time you. But if you're alone right now, don't put this investigation off. Do it yourself. Wait until the second hand is up at the twelve. Then close your eyes. When you think ten seconds is up, open your eyes and quickly look at where the second hand is.

How did you do? Did ten seconds take longer than you had imagined or less time? Or did you estimate just about right? (How close would your estimate have to be to be just about right?)

Just How Long Is a Second?

If you know a bit about fractions, you can figure out how long a second is. A second is 1/60 of a minute, which is 1/60 of an hour, which is 1/24 of a day. So a second is 1/86,400 of a day.

This was the first definition of a second. It was used for a long while, until astronomers noticed that each day wasn't exactly the same length. The spin of the earth varies. It's slower one day and faster the next. The difference between one day and the next isn't very much, maybe a few thousandths of a second. But it's enough to make scientists feel uncomfortable.

In 1820, a committee of French scientists had an idea. Let's say that the second is 1/86,400 of an average length day, they said. So they averaged the length of a year's worth of days and came up with a length of time that was called the mean solar day. The new definition was that a second was 1/86,400 of this mean solar day. This was the second definition of a second, and it stuck for more than a century.

Then scientists noticed something new. The earth doesn't only spin irregularly on its axis, it's also slowing down. It's not slowing down very much, about twenty micro-seconds a year. That's only twenty seconds every million years. But this means the length of time used for the mean solar day isn't accurate.

So, in 1956, the definition of a second was changed again. The decision was to figure the time of a second as a fraction of an average year instead of an average day. The year 1900 was chosen. This was called the mean solar year. The fraction is a complicated one; it even has a decimal in it. The second was now 1/31,556,925.9747 of that year. This was the third definition of the second.

But that definition didn't last long, either. In 1967, scientists decided that basing the length of a second on the motions of the earth just wasn't going to be good enough. Even the tiniest changes in those motions made their figuring inaccurate for the complex scientific discoveries that were being made.

Also, about this time, clocks had been perfected so they kept time with incredible accuracy. A modern atomic clock uses atoms of a metal called cesium to keep it in time. This type of clock is so accurate that if kept running for thirty-thousand years, it would be off by only one second. That's more reliable than the movements of the earth. Scientists felt that the stability of this type of clock should be what's used for defining time. After all, a second is really a length of time made up for human convenience. It was just an arbitrary decision for people to agree on a useful unit for measuring certain short lengths of time. So why not make it as accurate as possible for modern science?

Here's the fourth definition. The second is the time it takes for a cesium atom to vibrate in a certain way 9,192,631,770 times. To understand that totally, you'd have to understand more about the metal cesium and how it's used in atomic clocks. It's too complicated to explain here, but keep your ears open in your science classes at school.

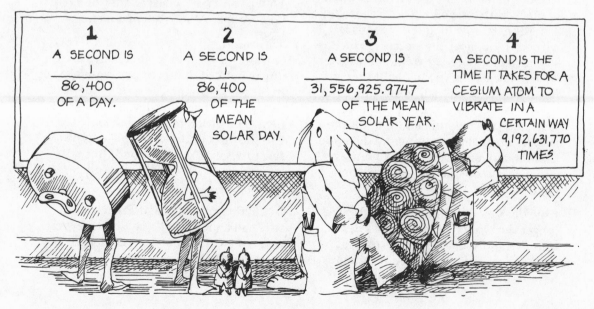

1 A SECOND IS $\frac{1}{86,400}$ OF A DAY.

2 A SECOND IS $\frac{1}{86,400}$ OF THE MEAN SOLAR DAY.

3 A SECOND IS $\frac{1}{31,556,925.9747}$ OF THE MEAN SOLAR YEAR.

4 A SECOND IS THE TIME IT TAKES FOR A CESIUM ATOM TO VIBRATE IN A CERTAIN WAY 9,192,631,770 TIMES.

The Ping-Pong Second

Do you play Ping-Pong? If your answer is yes, then try this experiment next time you're playing to get a feel for how long a second is. The idea is for you and a friend to hit the ball back and forth so each of you gets five hits. Don't use any of your fancy shots; just try to keep the ball in play. Try to time your rally so it takes ten seconds from the time the first person hits the ball until the other player's fifth shot is completed. Do you think this would be a fast rally or a slow one? Try it.

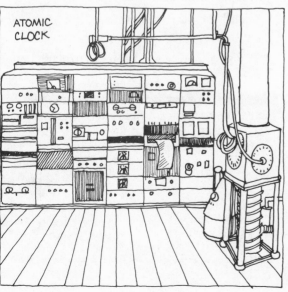

Leap Seconds

The year 1975 got a little extra time added to it — one extra second. You can think of it as a "leap" second. It was added on December 31, 1975, so the new year would get started on time.

What is this all about? Atomic clocks, which are the official timekeepers, keep better time than the earth does. There was a slight slowdown in the earth's rotation in 1975. Adding a leap second is like stopping the clock for one second so the earth can catch up with it and then starting the clock up again.

Not just the United States added the leap second, most of the countries in the world did — at least those that coordinate their official time together and are members of the International Committee of Weights and Measures.

This wasn't the first time a leap second was added, either. The very first time was at the end of June, 1972. It was the first official minute with sixty-one seconds in history. Since then, leap seconds have been added whenever they've been needed. You probably never noticed.

How Is Your Reaction Time?

Your reaction time is a measure of how fast your body answers a signal. Here's where seconds can be a useful time measure. You can try some experiments with a friend to test how fast your own reactions are.

Reaction Experiment One: This experiment tests both your reaction time and your friend's reaction time. It's a game. One of you puts your hands on the palms of the other person. The idea is for the player on the bottom to try to move their hands fast enough to try to slap the top of the other person's hands. And the player on top tries to get their hands away before getting slapped. The bottom player scores a point each time they slap either or both of the other person's hands. Whenever the bottom player misses, change positions so the bottom player puts their hands on top and vice versa. Play until someone scores eleven.

Reaction Experiment Two: This tests just one person's reaction time. Take turns doing it so you both get a chance. You need a twelve-inch ruler or a strip of cardboard marked off in inches or centimeters. One person holds the ruler straight up and down at the top edge. The other person puts their hand just at the bottom of the ruler without

touching it, but waiting to catch it as it falls through their fingers. The person holding the ruler is going to drop it without saying when. The other person is going to try to catch it. See how far down the ruler falls before it is caught. Do this several times to see if you can improve your reaction time.

Some people think that this experiment is easy, until they actually try it. As a matter of fact, one person thought that it was so easy, it cost them one dollar to find out how hard it really was. That's because the person who knew better made this deal: "I bet that if you give me a dollar, and I hold it at the top and your fingers are waiting to catch it at the bottom, you'll miss it when I drop it."

"Nah," the other person said, "that's dumb. Of course I'll catch it."

"If you miss it, can I keep the dollar?"

The second person agreed. Guess what happened, or try it yourself. But make sure your reaction time is fast enough to get away with the dollar before the other person changes their mind.

It May Not Be Funny, But It's Fast

Ever hit your funny bone? What you feel is an automatic reaction. Your whole arm tingles and feels strange. What you've done is hit your ulnar nerve. It runs from your spine down each of your arms. When you bash your elbow and set off that sensation, it takes only 2/100 of a second for the feeling to get to your hand. That is hardly any time at all, much less at all funny. Why do you think it's called the funny bone, anyway?

How Much Time Does a Blink Take?

How long is a blink? A second? More than that? Less than that? Look at the word below. Then blink. Does it seem to disappear at all for the time when your eyes are closed? Try it again.

HELLO

You can figure out how long a blink is two different ways. Try both of them. Then you can compare the results. Before you try either, make a guess about how long you think a blink really is.

Here are the two ways to measure a blink.

Blink Measure Number One: You need a friend and a watch or clock with a second hand. Ask your friend to say "Go" when they start timing. Then you blink ten times, counting the blinks out loud. Your friend should figure out how many seconds it took from "Go" until you said "Ten." Divide that time by ten, and you'll have the time of one of your blinks.

Blink Measure Number Two: In this method, your friend times a ten-second period. When they say "Go," you start blinking and count the number of blinks to yourself until your friend says "Stop." That should be after ten seconds has passed. Divide ten by the number of blinks to find out how long one blink was.

How did your results from these two methods compare? How far off was your guess?

Which Is Longer —
a Blink or a Squeeze?

If you've figured out how long one of your blinks is, then all you need to know to answer this question is how long a squeeze takes. An easy way to figure out the length of a squeeze is to wait until you have a bunch of people together. The more people, the better your figuring will be. Here's how to do it.

One of the people is the timer. That person will need a clock or a watch with a second hand. The rest of the people should join hands in a circle. Sitting so you all face out is a good way to help people concentrate on their squeezes.

Decide which person in the circle will be the squeeze starter. You also need to decide before starting how many times you'll send the squeeze around the group. This depends on how many people you've got squeezing. A total of at least ten squeezes is good; more is bet-

ter. So if you've got three or four people in the circle, send the squeezes around three times. For five to ten people, send the squeezes around twice. For more than that, once around the circle is enough.

When you've got that figured, you're ready to start. When the timer says "Go," the starter starts the squeeze in one direction. Each person squeezes their neighbor's hand right after they feel a squeeze. When the squeeze gets back to the starter the first time, it has gone around once. If it needs to go around more, the starter should just keep the squeeze moving. When it's gone around the number of times you first agreed on and it's back to the starter, the starter should say "Stop."

The timer tells how many seconds it took. Divide that number by the number of squeezes to figure the time of one squeeze. Well, which is longer — a blink or a squeeze?

Slicing the Second

A second may seem like a short enough division of time for you, but there are times when people need to slice a second into much tinier bits. At track meets, for instance, races are clocked to tenths of a second. In close races, photo-finish cameras can show time in hundredths of a second.

Some people need to measure time in even smaller bits than that — in milliseconds or microseconds or nanoseconds or even picoseconds. Have you ever heard of these?

A millisecond is one thousandth of a second. Photographers use cameras with shutters that can open for just that length of time. That's how they can get a clear photo of something that's moving rapidly.

A microsecond is one millionth of a second. When ship captains are navigating through heavy fog, they need to have time measured down to microseconds to be absolutely sure of the position of the ship. This can be a matter of life and death.

A nanosecond is one billionth of a second. Some computers can carry out a thousand million calculations in one second. That's an average of one calculation each nanosecond.

A picosecond is one trillionth of a second. Physicists use this measure of time when studying particles that are produced by atom smashers.

Watching a Split Second

Here's a way to actually see times that are less than a second. Find someone whose hobby is photography and who has a camera that has adjustable shutter speeds. The next time the camera doesn't have any film in it, ask the owner to open the back so you can see forward through the camera to the lens. Then ask the owner to click the camera at different shutter speeds so you can see the light come through the lens. That will give you an interesting view of bits of time.

Some cameras have shutter speeds of 1/30, 1/60, or 1/100 of a second. More expensive cameras have shutter speeds from one second all the way to 1/1000 of a second. You'll need to watch closely to see the light come through at the very fastest speeds.

Which of those shutter speeds is about the same length of time as one of your blinks? If you're interested, ask the owner to explain why different shutter speeds are useful.

CLOSED SHUTTER   OPEN SHUTTER

How Long Are Sounds?

When you drop a book, how long does the sound it makes when it hits the floor last? Or how long does it take for the book to hit? Can you devise experiments to measure these bits of time?

When a baseball bat hits a ball, the impact lasts only 2/1000 of a second. Yet that bit of time is pretty important when it's a close game.

Speeding Up for Slow Motion

Maybe you've seen what movie film looks like. It's a long strip made up of little separate pictures. When a filmmaker shoots that film, the camera usually takes all those separate pictures at the rate of twenty-four frames per second. And when the film is developed and projected so you can watch it, the action looks like normal motion all in one continuous flow.

But suppose a filmmaker wants to make part of a film in slow motion. Then the speed that the movie camera takes those separate little pictures has to be changed. Which way do you think the camera is adjusted? Does it now click fewer pictures in a second or more pictures in a second. Try thinking about that.

If you guessed that the camera is set to click more pictures each second, you were right. How it's really done is that the camera is speeded up, so instead of taking twenty-four pictures each second, it takes up to sixty-four pictures each second. How does speeding up the film like this make slow motion? Well, when the film is shown, the projector runs the film through at the same speed as all other film, twenty-four frames each second. So it takes two and a half seconds to show the same sequence that would have taken only one second if it had been shot at the regular speed. The motion gets spread out over time. Speeding up the shooting and keeping the projector's speed steady is what produces slow motion.

Just the opposite is true for those movies when everyone seems to be zooming around the screen at breakneck speed, with funny jerking motions. That kind of footage is shot at only twelve frames per second. Remember, the projector shows all the film at the same speed, so this one compresses the action into those fast, funny-looking scenes.

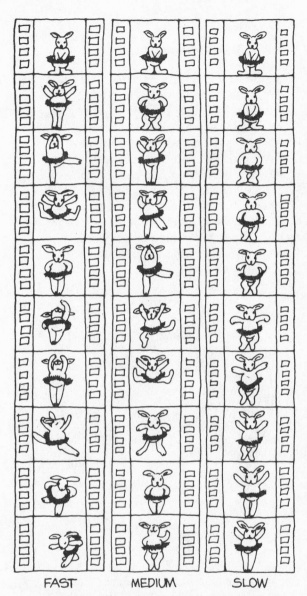

FAST   MEDIUM   SLOW

The Telephone Talking Clock

In most places in the United States, you can dial a special telephone number and find out what time it is. Check the front of your telephone book or in the yellow pages under Time of Day or Time-Temperature to find out if you can do this where you live. The number will be listed there. If you have the service, you can call anytime, day or night, and hear what time it is. You'll never even get a busy signal.

If you've never tried it, look up the number and dial it. The message may vary slightly, depending on where you live, but it will sound close to one of these: "The time is 3:42 and 10 seconds. . . BEEP," or "At the tone the time will be 11:23 exactly. . .BEEP."

There's no use trying to have a conversation with the person telling you the time. She won't talk back. What you hear when you dial is a recording, which is a good thing. Imagine what a boring job it would be if somebody had to sit there all day and night telling the time out loud. Besides, no one could ever do it as accurately as the telephone talking clock does.

SO, HOW'S YOUR FAMILY B... HEY! DON'T INTERRUPT ME AGAIN!

Who Knows the Exact Time, Anyway?

The National Bureau of Standards keeps track of the exact time for the United States. That's done in two places: Fort Collins, Colorado, and on the island of Kauai in Hawaii. At each of those places, a radio station transmits time signals that tell the exact official time.

Atomic clocks have been used to keep this official time since the last day of January, 1971. Since that time, the United States has been on atomic time.

How Exact Is the Talking Clock?

The talking clock is incredibly exact, especially if your telephone service is from one of these large cities in the United States: Los Angeles, New York, Chicago, Detroit, San Francisco, Boston, Washington, D. C., or Baltimore. The equipment in these cities is hooked up to one of the official U. S. Bureau of Standard's timepieces.

The talking clock time in the large cities is continually compared with the official time by radio signals sent from the official timekeepers. If there is any drift in the telephone clock, it will be automatically corrected. The talking clock will lose only fifty milliseconds a year. That's a loss of one second every twenty years. And that's probably as exact as you'll ever need.

If you don't live near one of those big cities, don't worry. The talking clock you hear isn't hooked up to the official U. S. timekeeper, but it's checked regularly. The time message you get won't be off more than thirty seconds a month. That's probably as exact as you'll ever need too.

Who Does the Talking?

If you have the time service where you live, you probably hear Jane Barbe's voice on the talking clock. She has a very well-known voice, even though most of the people who hear her talk have never seen her and have no idea who she is. She's been recording announcements for Audichron Company for over fifteen years. Through these recordings, Jane Barbe talks to more people in one day than any other human in the world — about twenty million people daily.

JANE BARBE

David and Susan are Jane Barbe's children. They're teenagers and live with their parents in Georgia. They admit that they do get teased about their mom's job sometimes, especially when someone happens to ask what time it is.

It only takes Jane Barbe one hour to record what's needed to tell the time throughout the twenty-four hour day. That's because she records the message in three separate parts. One part gives the hours, one part gives the minutes, and one part gives the seconds. Here's how it's done.

The hours first: Jane Barbe records all that is needed for the hours in twelve parts. She says, "The time is one," and stops. Then she says, "The time is two," and stops again. And she keeps going all the way to "The time is twelve."

Then the minutes part: She has sixty of those parts to do, from one to fifty-nine, plus she has to record "o'clock" for when the time is just on the hour.

The third part Jane Barbe records is the seconds. These are done in ten-second intervals, so she only has six different ones to say: "and ten seconds," up to "and fifty seconds" and the sixth one is "exactly."

An hour later, after recording all that, Jane Barbe goes home, and the Audichron Company is left with all these bits and pieces. Those pieces are installed on special magnetic drums which coordinate those three parts of the time recording that Jane Barbe made. When you hear it on the telephone, they sound like one complete message.

How About Your House Clocks?

Call that time number again and check to see how accurate the clocks in your house are. Maybe your timekeepers could use a little regular time checking that the telephone talking clock can help you with.

How Long Does It Take You to Read a Word?

Before you read the next section, get a clock or watch with a second hand so you can time yourself. There are three hundred words in the next section, not counting the title. Read it at your normal reading speed. Time when you start and when you finish. Then figure how many seconds it took you to read it. Divide three hundred by the number of seconds you took. That will tell you how many words you read in one second. Then you can figure how long it takes you to read one word.

FORTUNATELY, THIS ISN'T THE WAY THE TALKING CLOCK WORKS.

AT THE SOUND OF THE TONE THE TIME WILL BE FOUR FIFTEEN AND FIFTY SECONDS.

RING! RING! RING! RING!

63

The Tale of the Telephone Operator

There was a woman who was the only telephone operator in a small town. She did most of the work that is done automatically today. This was before there were any telephone talking clocks and when the sun was the chief timekeeper. So she did that job along with everything else. But it wasn't a big part of her work. Hardly anyone ever called her to check the time, except for one man. He'd phone late in the morning and ask this telephone operator for the time. She'd check her watch and tell him what the time was. This happened every day she worked.

Finally the woman was about to retire. She had been the telephone operator in this town for about thirty years. The time had come for her to quit. On her last day of work, the man called as usual. She felt she owed it to him to say goodbye. Besides that, she had been curious for a while about his daily call.

So when he called, she told him the time as she always did. "But before you hang up," she also said, "I'd like to tell you that this is my last day on the job. And I've been wondering about something all these years that I've been here. How come you call every day at the same time, just before lunch, and ask me what time it is?"

He answered her with a question. "Do you know that every day the noon whistle gets sounded over at the firehouse?"

"Yes," she said. Everyone in town could hear the noon whistle.

"That's my job," he went on, "and I call you to check the time so I know when it's noon."

"Oh, dear," she said, "I've been setting my watch by that noon whistle all these years."

Chapter 6
The Calendar Story

What do you think of when you think about a calendar? Do you picture all those months, neatly divided into squares, with the dates clearly marked? Do you think of it as a way to keep track of your birthday? Do you use it as a system for knowing when it's Halloween time or Thanksgiving or summer vacation? Does a calendar tell you whether it's a school day or a weekend day?

Maybe you really don't think about the calendar very much. Most people don't, except at the end of the year when they realize that they need a new one. The calendar is just there — and a good thing too. It helps most people keep their lives organized. Think about how you do use a calendar to keep your life sorted.

Suppose there were no calendars for keeping track of time. How would that change people's lives? How would that change your life?

The calendar does have some funny quirks. You need to memorize that "Thirty Days Hath September" poem to remember how many days there are in each month. Then there's February — the weird month of the bunch. But the calendar does the job of keeping track of time during the year.

That nice orderly calendar you use was no easy feat to put together. It's taken people thousands of years to figure it out, and it's still not perfect. Keep reading and you'll learn why. Not even the same calendar is used all over the world. You'll find out about that too. Then there are some people who think that the calendar is just a mess and needs to be totally reorganized to make good time sense. You'll learn about that and what those people have in mind.

The First Calendar Clues

People had some specific needs for keeping track of time thousands of years ago. They needed to know when it was time to plant seeds. They needed to know when certain religious holidays came. These needs sparked the search for an organized calendar, but how did people start this search? Can you imagine what you would have done if the job had been yours?

There were clues that people in ancient times found around them. The sun was one clue. It was a reliable way of watching time. People counted off the days by suns. But that didn't help tell which day was the one to get out and start the year's planting or which was the right day for a religious holiday.

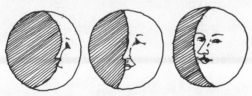

Then there was the moon. That was another reliable time clue. People noticed that the cycle of change from new moon to full moon and back to new moon was a regular occurrence. When they counted the days, they learned that the sun appeared twenty-nine times between one full moon and the next.

They counted again. This time it took thirty days for the full moon to come around again. After checking this out, they found that the moon's phases averaged about twenty-nine and a half days. Now that's not such a convenient number for calendar making, but it was a start. It's not the same length of time as the months used today, but it's pretty close. Maybe the twenty-nine and a half days of the moon's cycle should be called a "moonth." But they're not — they're called a lunar month.

The Babylonians Use the Moon

The ancient Babylonians set up a calendar using these lunar months. Their system got them in timekeeping trouble. Their year had twelve lunar months, which adds up to 354 days. They didn't know about the 365 days it takes for the earth to make a complete trip around the sun. So when they picked the month to do the planting, next year that same month came about a little earlier according to the seasons. If they continued with this system, after several years, they'd be out there in the middle of winter trying to turn the soil, and that would be dumb.

66

The Babylonians noticed this, and they fixed it. They just added some extra days to their calendar to avoid that catastrophe. Adding extra time like that to a calendar is called intercalation. That's what's done today when an extra day is added on to leap years.

Moon Watching

Have you ever paid close attention to the phases of the moon? Make this a month's project and check out what the Babylonians discovered.

Take a look at the moon every other night for a complete cycle. You can start any day you'd like, but it's especially nice to start this project on the night when there's a new moon. You· can check this on a calendar or in the newspaper.

First collect fifteen index cards that are three by five inches. Set up the project by putting each date you will observe the moon on the left half of a card. Putting the day can also help remind you when to go out and look.

Every night that's marked on the cards, take a careful look at the moon. If you have binoculars, use them. Draw the shape of the moon in the circle on the right side of the card. Use the circle that's there as a guide.

If it's cloudy or rainy one night and the moon isn't visible, check it the next night. Then stay on the schedule you made. When you're done with the cycle, put all the cards in order. Hold them on the left side, riffle through them, and watch the phases go by quickly.

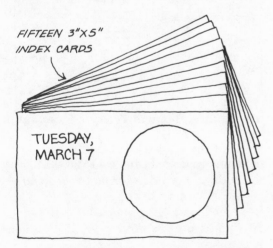

FIFTEEN 3"X5" INDEX CARDS

TUESDAY, MARCH 7

On the right side of each card, draw a circle lightly in pencil. Use a compass to make it or trace around the bottom of a glass or jar. The circles should be about two inches in diameter.

The Egyptians Turn to the Stars

The ancient Egyptians used a different clue when they designed their calendar. They noticed that the stars moved across the night sky in a regular pattern. The brightest star you can see is called Sirius, and that's the one they focused on. The Egyptian astronomers would watch for the time each year when Sirius first appeared on the horizon in the morning.

They knew that happened every 365 days. They also knew that the appearance of Sirius meant the floods were on their way and that planting could begin soon after. They marked the beginning of a new year with the reappearance of Sirius.

They divided the year into twelve 30-day months. That made 360 days. Then they tacked on 5 extra days at the end of the year to make 365. Those were feast days to celebrate the birthdays of five gods.

The Egyptian calendar hit a snag, though. Every fourth year, Sirius appeared one day late. That's because the year is really 365¼ days long. The Egyptian astronomers knew this, and they predicted the flood correctly. But they never did change the calendar. So after many years, the calendar was way off base.

The Mayas Had the Answer

In Central America over two thousand years ago, the Mayas had it all figured out. They made it their business not to get all confused about measuring time. Time was so important to their religion that they were careful enough to do it right.

They kept exact observations of the sun and the moon and the stars. Priest-astronomers kept separate records on each of these three time-telling guides in almanacs or on tall stone pillars. Then they would check the three different records against each other. That way they knew when their special religious days occurred and when to plant and harvest.

The Mayas divided their year into eighteen months, with 20 days in each month. That accounted for 360 days. They also added on 5 more days to make the 365-day year, but they weren't holidays, though, like the Egyptian extra days were. These were considered to be bad luck days, kind of like having 5 Friday-the-13ths all in a row. The Mayas also figured out a clever formula for including that extra one-quarter of a day in their records. The Mayan calendar was more exact than the one you use today.

The Roman Roots of Today's Calendar

None of these calendar attempts had anything to do with the calendar you use today. Ours comes from the Roman calendar, though lots of changes have been made in it over the past twenty-five hundred years or so to get it where it is today.

The first Roman calendar was a lunar calendar. There were ten months: Martius, Aprilis, Maius, Junius, Quintilis, Sextilis, September, October, November, and December. Look familiar? What's missing, and what's different from today's calendar? Six of these months had thirty days; four of them had thirty-one days. Try guessing which were the thirty-one-day months.

So the year added up to 304 days. That's 61¼ days short of a full year. The priests responsible for telling time knew about this shortage. They fixed it by not announcing the new year in Martius until it was the right time. Those extra days were there in the dead of winter when nothing much seemed to be happening anyway, so they just didn't count them.

Back to the thirty-one-day months. Those four were Martius, Maius, Quintilis, and October. Did you guess right?

Numa's New Additions

King Numa was one of the leaders of ancient Rome. One thing he did in his rule was to try to fix the calendar. In about 712 B.C., he had two more months added to the calendar, just before Martius. They were called Januarius and Februarius. He did some more fiddling with the calendar too. He changed the lengths of some of the months.

It seems that even numbers were thought to be unlucky numbers to the Romans. So Emperor Numa made all the 30-day months 29-day months. He made Januarius 29 days also, but made Februarius a 28-day month. Februarius was an oddball month even way back then. By giving Februarius 28 days, he made the total number of days in the year an odd number instead of an even number. The year was now 355 days. That wasn't an unlucky number. It was just wrong. The Emperor's calendar experts pointed this out to him. "Listen," they said, "we're short about 22 days every two years."

That didn't bother the Emperor. His solution was intercalation. "So add an extra 22-day month every two years," he said. It seems that Emperors could do just about anything. But the experts weren't so expert. Those 22 days didn't make good calendar sense. They made each year 11 days longer, which brought it up to 366 days. Not good.

The Caesars Get in the Calendar Picture

By the time Julius Caesar came into power, the calendar was a total mess. Not only was the plan wrong, but the priest-astronomers didn't even follow their plan regularly. It was a calendar disaster.

"Enough of this," was Julius Caesar's opinion. In the year 46 B.C., he decided to get this calendar back in line with the seasons and figure a way to keep it in line with the seasons. The new plan was called the Julian calendar. It had twelve months, starting with Januarius. The months were thirty or thirty-one days long. Except for Februarius, of course. An extra day was added every four years, just like today. What a relief. Caesar was proud of this reform. He was so proud that he made one more change. The month that used to be called Quintilis (check the names on page 68) was changed. Now it was to be called Julius. Here's how the calendar stood:

JANUARIUS	31 DAYS
FEBRUARIUS	29 DAYS *
MARTIUS	31 DAYS
APRILIS	30 DAYS
MAIUS	31 DAYS
JUNIUS	30 DAYS
JULIUS	31 DAYS
SEXTILIS	30 DAYS
SEPTEMBER	31 DAYS
OCTOBER	30 DAYS
NOVEMBER	31 DAYS
DECEMBER	30 DAYS

* EXCEPT 30 EVERY FOURTH YEAR

Compare that with today's calendar. There are some differences in the lengths of the months. Can you find them? And there's one difference in the names of the months. That Sextilis. Today it's called August.

This is because of the next emperor after Julius Caesar. His name was Caesar Augustus. Get the hint? He wasn't going to get the short end of the calendar changing. Not only did a month get named after him, it got an extra day added so his month had as many days as Julius Caesar's month did. The extra day was taken from Februarius, which seems to get pushed around a lot. In the shuffle, the days in the last four months were switched too.

All was fine for a long, long time — for over fifteen hundred years. Then a problem that had been building all those years demanded some attention. What was this problem? Well, it turns out that the year really isn't exactly 365¼ days long. It's just a little bit shorter than that.

A 365¼-day year would be 365 days and six hours. But the actual year is only 365 days, five hours, forty-eight minutes and forty-six seconds long, give or take a bit. The Julian calendar year was a little over eleven minutes too long. And eleven minutes a year can add up. The calendar was out of whack with the seasons again.

Pope Gregory Cleans Up the Calendar

Pope Gregory XIII decided to get the calendar back in step in 1582. By that time, those eleven minutes a year had added up to ten days' worth. So Pope Gregory had ten days cut out of the calendar. He did this on October 4, 1582. On October 4, he just ripped ten days off the calendar instead of one. Then next came October 15, instead of October 5.

WAIT! YOUR HOLINESS, THAT'S MY BIRTHDAY!!

To stop this accumulation of days from happening again, Pope Gregory changed the leap-year rule. The rule had been that all the years that could be divided evenly by four were leap years. The new rule applied to all years except the century years: 1600, 1700, 1800, 1900, 2000, and so on. In order for those to be leap years, they have to be divisible by four hundred instead of by four. This eliminates some of them. Now this new calendar, the Gregorian calendar, is off by only twenty-six seconds a year, which means it will only go out of step one day every 3,323 years. That won't happen until the year 4905. Then the nearest leap day will have to be dropped. How old will you be in the year 4905? Do you think you'll be around then?

It took some time for other countries to go along with Pope Gregory's changes. The Roman Catholic countries all adopted it immediately, but the European Protestant countries didn't do so until the 1700s. By that time, the old Julian calendar was eleven days off instead of ten. That's because by Pope Gregory's leap-year rule, 1700 didn't get an extra day because it can't be divided evenly by four hundred.

It was no easy switch in Great Britain. They waited until 1752 to make it. People were furious. "You're robbing us of time," some said. "We're going to lose almost two weeks rent," landlords complained. "We're losing wages," workers cried. A mob formed outside the Houses of Parliament shouting, "Give us back our eleven days! Give us back our eleven days!" But the change was made. After September 2, 1752, came September 14. And after a while, the fuss died down.

In 1752, Great Britain still controlled the American colonies, so the calendar change was made here too. Japan adopted it in 1873. China did in 1912. The Russians waited until 1918. Today, this is the calendar used for most business and daily dealings, even though other calendars are still used in various parts of the world. It's called the Gregorian calendar.

When Was the Cherry Tree Really Chopped Down?

What about birthdays when the calendar was changed? Some of those got changed too. George Washington was born on February 11, 1732, by the old Julian calendar. But on the new Gregorian calendar, his birthday is February 22, which is when we celebrate it. What do you think about that?

A Present That Lasts a Year

Calendars have become a booming business. Calendars are made each year for cat lovers, dog lovers, ski fans, for people who like the outdoors or butterflies or flowers. There are calendars that are full of riddles for every month or famous paintings or recipes or cartoon characters.

Some calendars are made to hang on the wall. Some sit on a desk. Some are postcards so when the month is over, you can tear it off and mail it to someone. There are even calendars that glow in the dark. That might be useful if you ever wake up in the middle of the night and just have to know what the date is.

You can buy calendars in bookstores. You can often get them free from banks. But Patrick and Paul had another idea. They decided to make their dad a calendar for Christmas, and they did it in a very special way.

They decided to design something special for each month. They used both photographs of themselves and drawings they had made. Each boy designed the month that his birthday was in. They put one of their school photos in the middle of the page and decorated around it. They saved some snapshots of themselves in their Halloween costumes and used those for the month of October. For the other months, they collected their favorite drawings.

Their mom helped them by keeping a pad of good drawing paper in one special place for a few months before Christmas. Whenever they felt a special drawing coming on, they'd do it in the good pad. That way, when they got to putting their calendar together, they had a whole selection of good art to choose from.

Their mom also helped them put it all together. Here's how. First they took seven manila file folders and cut off the tabs. They put the folders together, one inside the other, like a book. They turned their book sideways and all their decorations went on the top half of each page. The bottom half was ruled carefully for each month. Using another calendar as a sample helps to do this. They marked not only the holidays on the right dates but family birthdays too.

By punching holes on the folds, they were able to tie the folders together. Patrick and Paul used a piece of leather, but yarn or ribbon would work just as well.

Their dad was really pleased when he got it. Mostly because it was a nice reminder of the boys, and it was a present that would last all year long.

The Wavering Week

What about the week? Where does that fit into the calendar story? The week didn't always have seven days. The ancient Greeks used a ten-day week. The Romans had eight days of market and one day of rest. To have seven days in a week is another of those time decisions that just happened and stuck.

But there are a couple of reasons why seven days seemed reasonable. One has to do with the moon. Remember, the moon goes through a regular cycle that takes about twenty-nine and a half days to complete. Each of the four phases, from new moon to half moon or from half moon to full moon, takes a little more than seven days. The ancient Babylonians noticed this and used a seven-day division because of it.

A seven-day week has always been important to Jewish people. That's because to Jews the seventh day has a special religious meaning as the day of rest, the Sabbath. The first book in the Old Testament of the Bible, the Book of Genesis, tells about that. That feature of Jewish timekeeping has stuck and spread.

There have been attempts to change the week from time to time. Some of these made some big-time splashes in history.

France Goes Scientific

One attempt to change the week was made in France in 1792. That's when a big scientific effort was made to straighten out time once and for all. The week was changed to ten days, a nice decimal number that fit in well with the metric system. It wasn't only the week that was reorganized at that time. The whole calendar was, making changes in the months and years.

The day was changed too. It was divided into ten hours, with one hundred minutes in each hour. How many seconds do you think there were in each minute? It was one hundred. It all seemed tidy, from a reasonable scientific position. But the people were in an uproar.

Imagine getting used to hours that felt different and minutes and seconds that were longer. Imagine making all new clocks. Can you imagine either of those? And it seemed antireligious to some. What would happen to church on Sundays, not to say what would happen to the names of the days of the week, anyway.

It didn't last long, that time idea. Dividing the day into ten hours with their one hundred minutes and one hundred seconds went under in 1795. And the rest of the changes, including the ten-day week, were given up in 1806. At that time, France went back to the seven-day week.

The Soviet Union Tries Something Different

In 1929, the Soviet Union changed from the Gregorian calendar. They tried a five-day week. What they planned was four days of work and one day of rest for people. But not everyone had the same day of rest. That meant that all stores and factories and other businesses could be open all the time since workers had different days off.

The days of the week didn't have names, they had colors: yellow, orange, red, purple, and green. All the workers were assigned a color that told them which was their day of rest. Things got much too confusing. Special arrangements had to be made so families could have recreation time together. Friends had problems. If you were a yellow and your friend was a purple, there was no way you could go off together one day for a picnic.

So in 1932, they changed this five-day-week plan. This time they tried six days. That meant five days of work and one day of rest. Everyone had the same day off. It seemed okay, except then it was noticed that way out in the countryside, people didn't pay much attention to this wavering week. They had ignored the five-day plan and were ignoring the six-day plan. They just got on with their lives and their work, usually on the old seven-day plan.

It was mostly in the cities that the changes happened. But all the people who had jobs that included working with foreign countries had to use the regular seven-day week anyway. Finally on June 27, 1940, the Soviet Union joined the rest of the world. They decided on the seven-day week and went back to using the Gregorian calendar.

The Week Stands at Seven

So here you are, living a seven-day week. Have you ever thought that it might be a good idea to change it? How about an eight-day week so you could have a three-day weekend from school? Maybe a shorter one, so you would go to school for three days and then have two days at home. What do you think would be the ideal week for you?

There are some people who think that the way the week is organized isn't the best way for working and playing. Some of these people think that they'd rather work more than five days in a row if they could have more than a two-day break. Some people today work a four-day week, usually longer days, so they can have a three-day break. Check around with the grownups you know and ask their opinions about an ideal week and how it would be organized.

Unless some change is made, you'll go on living with the week that has seven days, 168 hours, 10,080 minutes, and 604,800 seconds.

Measuring Time by Olympiads

In ancient Greece, the Olympic games were so important that they were used as the markers of time. The games were held every four years then, just as they are now. The first one was in 776 B.C. (Do you know when the next Olympic games will be held?)

Every year that the games were held marked the beginning of an Olympiad. Each Olympiad was four years long. Instead of saying that Alexander the Great died in 323 B.C., the Greeks said that Alexander the Great died in the second year of the 114th Olympiad.

The Big Calendar Complaint

There's another calendar, called the World Calendar, that has been proposed. This calendar was figured out by the World Calendar Association. That organization was founded in 1930 and has been working since then to change the Gregorian calendar.

Why do they want to do this? What's so wrong with the calendar used today? The World Calendar Association thinks that there is lots wrong with the Gregorian calendar. There are inconsistencies, they say. It's not logical or reliable. Here are some of the problems they cite.

Problem One: The months have four different lengths: twenty-eight, twenty-nine, thirty, and thirty-one days. This means all kids have to learn that "Thirty Days Hath September" poem. Or they have to learn the knuckle method of remembering which month has how many days. Do you know that method?

The Knuckle Method of Months

Make a fist. Say the months in order, pointing to your knuckles and the spaces in between. Say January and point to a knuckle, February, point to a space. And so on. The months that land on the knuckles all have thirty-one days. Remember when you get to July to go back to where you started on your hand, so August falls on a knuckle. You just have to remember about February.

Problem Two: No date ever lands on the same day of the week in two consecutive years. So if your birthday is on a Tuesday this year, it won't be on a Tuesday next year. That doesn't seem like a terrible problem for birthdays, but wouldn't it be nice if Halloween fell on the same day every year, like on a Friday, so you wouldn't have to go to bed early to get up for school the next morning?

Problem Three: A year or a month can begin on any of the seven days of the week. That's because there are 52 weeks in a year, but 52 times 7 equals 364. The extra day causes this inconsistency. It causes things like school starting every year on a different date and ending on a different date too. Does this mean you get a shorter summer vacation sometimes?

Problem Four: Because a month can start on any day of the week, there are twenty-eight different kinds of month patterns that can appear on calendars. This means that all months won't have the same number of workdays or school days. Another of those inconsistencies. There might be twenty-four school days in some months and as many as twenty-seven in others. Take a look at this year's calendar to see if that's so.

Problem Five: Suppose you were trying to figure out what day of the week a special holiday, like Martin Luther King, Jr.'s birthday, would land on some year in the future. Too complicated. Too much figuring.

All in all, the members of the World Calendar Association think that our calendar is just too irregular to be as useful as it could be. They think it could be organized better so that everything would be more orderly and predictable. Then no one would have the problem of being born on February 29 and only having a real birthday every four years. Do you know anyone with that birthday? What do they do about it?

The Suggested Solution

How does the World Calendar Association want to change the calendar? They propose a new calendar that looks like this:

THE WORLD CALENDAR

	JANUARY	FEBRUARY	MARCH
	S M T W T F S	S M T W T F S	S M T W T F S
	1 2 3 4 5 6 7	1 2 3 4	1 2
FIRST	8 9 10 11 12 13 14	5 6 7 8 9 10 11	3 4 5 6 7 8 9
QUARTER	15 16 17 18 19 20 21	12 13 14 15 16 17 18	10 11 12 13 14 15 16
	22 23 24 25 26 27 28	19 20 21 22 23 24 25	17 18 19 20 21 22 23
	29 30 31	26 27 28 29 30	24 25 26 27 28 29 30

	APRIL	MAY	JUNE
	S M T W T F S	S M T W T F S	S M T W T F S
	1 2 3 4 5 6 7	1 2 3 4	1 2
SECOND	8 9 10 11 12 13 14	5 6 7 8 9 10 11	3 4 5 6 7 8 9
QUARTER	15 16 17 18 19 20 21	12 13 14 15 16 17 18	10 11 12 13 14 15 16
	22 23 24 25 26 27 28	19 20 21 22 23 24 25	17 18 19 20 21 22 23
	29 30 31	26 27 28 29 30	24 25 26 27 28 29 30 W

	JULY	AUGUST	SEPTEMBER
	S M T W T F S	S M T W T F S	S M T W T F S
	1 2 3 4 5 6 7	1 2 3 4	1 2
THIRD	8 9 10 11 12 13 14	5 6 7 8 9 10 11	3 4 5 6 7 8 9
QUARTER	15 16 17 18 19 20 21	12 13 14 15 16 17 18	10 11 12 13 14 15 16
	22 23 24 25 26 27 28	19 20 21 22 23 24 25	17 18 19 20 21 22 23
	29 30 31	26 27 28 29 30	24 25 26 27 28 29 30

	OCTOBER	NOVEMBER	DECEMBER
	S M T W T F S	S M T W T F S	S M T W T F S
	1 2 3 4 5 6 7	1 2 3 4	1 2
FOURTH	8 9 10 11 12 13 14	5 6 7 8 9 10 11	3 4 5 6 7 8 9
QUARTER	15 16 17 18 19 20 21	12 13 14 15 16 17 18	10 11 12 13 14 15 16
	22 23 24 25 26 27 28	19 20 21 22 23 24 25	17 18 19 20 21 22 23
	29 30 31	26 27 28 29 30	24 25 26 27 28 29 30 W

W INDICATES WORLDSDAY, A WORLD HOLIDAY, AND EQUALS DECEMBER 31 (365TH DAY), WHICH FOLLOWS DECEMBER 30 EVERY YEAR. IN LEAP YEARS A SECOND WORLDSDAY IS ADDED AND EQUALS JUNE 31.

These are the different features of this calendar.

1. The year has exactly fifty-two weeks. That adds up to 364 days. An extra day comes at the end of December, called Worldsday, or December W. It's a holiday to be celebrated all over the world.

2. The leap-year day added every four years goes at the end of June. It's called Leap Year Day, or June W. It's another world holiday.

3. Every year begins on Sunday, the first day of January.

4. Every month has twenty-six weekdays, plus Sundays. They're fixed so that your birthday comes on the same day of the week every year for your entire life.

5. The year is divided into four equal quarters.

6. Holidays will fall consistently on the same days, and dates and won't be roaming about the calendar.

77

Besides all these well-ordered mathematical solutions, it's something that everyone in the world can participate in. It can be a way to help promote world cooperation and friendship.

There have been arguments on both sides about this calendar. Some religious groups feel that it violates the Bible's rule of "The seventh day. . . thou shalt not do any work." They feel that Worldsday would throw the weeks all out of kilter. Other people say that holding on to old ways just because we're used to them doesn't make any sense when we could have a calendar that would work every year from now on.

What do you think? Are you ready to become a supporter of this suggested world calendar?

One More Idea

This search for the perfect calendar has been going on for thousands of years. The sun and the moon and the stars seemed like such promising beginnings. But calendar makers have never been able to make one that works the way they want using those natural time measures. Those measures are just enough off to have kept calendar makers sharpening their pencils and making more adjustments for a long time. The world just isn't perfectly synchronized — another of those mysterious quirks about time.

There still may be changes on the calendar you use. But for now, your calendar does the job of keeping your life well scheduled.

A Time Check

How's your time sense doing? Here's one way to take a time check. Read through this list of things to do. On a piece of paper, list the time you think each of these things takes.

1. Saying "spaghetti and meat balls."
2. Writing your name.
3. Reciting the pledge of allegiance.
4. Finding the word "fracture" in the dictionary.
5. Counting to one thousand.
6. Counting to one million.
7. Playing a game of tick-tack-toe.
8. Singing "Row, Row, Row Your Boat" all the way through three times.
9. Eating a carrot until you swallow the last bit.
10. Convincing your parents you need an increase in your allowance.

Once you've predicted the times, devise an experiment to time each one. As you try each one, jot down how long it actually takes. How is your time sense doing?

Chapter 7
Nature's Amazing Clocks

How do plants know when it's time to start developing new buds? How do animals know when it's time to start growing their winter coats or to store up food for the cold time ahead? Birds head south in order to survive the winter. How do they know when to do this and where to go? Salmon need to know when it's time to head upstream and spawn. How do they tell time? How are desert creatures able to live in the heat of the sun during the day and also in the chill of midnight?

All living organisms on earth keep time. They don't keep time like you do with clocks or calendars. They've been doing their timekeeping since long before any human ever imagined the idea of a clock or calendar. Here's why.

The world runs on many different well-timed rhythms. These rhythms are regular cycles of change, and in order to survive, it has always been necessary for living things to keep in time with the earth's changes.

All living organisms have their own inner biological rhythms to help them exist in the world. These rhythms are their timekeeping methods. They're so powerful and so mysterious that they've fascinated people for a long, long time.

What are these internal rhythms in living things? Where do they come from? How are these inner clocks tuned into the rest of the world?

These are the questions that have tickled scientists' curiosities. They know that learning more about the biological cycles of all living organisms will help uncover more of the secrets about how the world works. Scientists are always probing for that kind of information.

Have you ever thought about all the time-keeping that's going on around you at every moment in the natural world? Here's your chance. This may be a brand new way for you to look at time in the world.

Telling the Time Without Clocks

Roosters get up early every day. They insist on announcing this, too, with their crowing. That daily cycle is hard to ignore if you've got a rooster for a neighbor. If you wanted to be sure to get up at sunrise every day, chances are that you would need an alarm clock. But roosters have their own clock — inside.

Australian flying foxes are nocturnal fruit bats. They spend their days hanging upside-down in the leaves of trees, sleeping. At dusk, they're good and hungry, so they fly out to feed at nearby fruit plantations. Australians who work on the plantations say that they always know when it is time to stop work each day. That's because the flying foxes arrive exactly on time every afternoon. If it weren't for these timely bats, the workers would have to depend on their watches.

A. S. Hudson was a physician who spent one summer taking care of cows. This was in the late 1800s. One thing he did regularly for the cows was to give them a weekly treat. He put out a salt stick on Sundays. Cows enjoy licking salt. Another thing he did regularly was to go out into the pasture to bring the cows in to be milked, except on Sundays. Then they'd all come in by themselves before he had a chance to go get them. They were waiting for the salt-stick treat. The cows seemed to know by themselves which day was Sunday. People need a calendar to keep track of days like that. How did the cows know?

Every year, swallows return from their winter home in South America to the mission at San Juan Capistrano in California. People often plan to go there to see them arrive. It's quite a sight. It's easy to plan when to go, because the swallows come just about March 19 every year. They do that without the help of a calendar.

The pileated tinamou is a bird that lives in Panama. It looks like a tiny ostrich. Most people who live there call it the three-hour bird. (That's lots easier to say than pileated tinamou.) Every three hours this bird sings, day and night. Some people in Panama believe you can set your watch by the song of the three-hour bird. Some have done checks with the airport clock and found that the birds are never more than a few minutes off. No one knows for sure why or how this bird's inner clock works.

These are five examples of what people have noticed about animals' and birds' time-telling abilities. These are the kinds of observations that have sparked people to study more. Have you any ideas yet about how any of these animals do their timekeeping? Keep reading, and you'll collect even more information.

Confusing the Clocks

On March 7, 1970, there was a total eclipse of the sun. It got suddenly dark during the day. Lots of animals were fooled. They thought nighttime was coming. In Florida it was reported that chickens went right to their roosts. Crickets started to chirp. Mosquitos, who are usually night pests, came right out and started munching on any humans they could find. What clue does this give you about what keeps some biological clocks running?

Fishing by the Clock

Hundreds of people in Southern California like to catch and eat grunion. Have you ever heard of grunion? They're little, thin, silvery fish, about as long as a man's hand. The internal rhythms of these fish make them simple to catch.

You can only catch grunion with your bare hands — that's the law. People who like to catch them know that there are only two times a month, from March to August, that they'll have any luck. As a matter of fact, people know exactly when those two times are. They're often announced on the radio or in the newspapers: "The grunion are expected to run tonight at 10:37." Have you ever heard of fishing like this? For any fish?

When the time is near, people all line the beach. They've got buckets or jars or sacks to fill. They stand patiently waiting. Kids play in the waves. All of a sudden, there's a change. Some of the people know that the tide has come in as far as it's going to and is starting to turn. They've only got to wait a few minutes more. They get their sacks ready. Then suddenly, a new wave breaks, and thousands of the silvery fish wash onto the beach. They've come up to deposit and fertilize their eggs.

The female grunion dances upright on her tail, digging herself down into the sand until half her body is buried. She sways back and forth and deposits her eggs in a hole three inches down. The male wriggles up, curves his body around hers, and fertilizes the eggs. Then they both slither back towards the water so the next wave will carry them back into the ocean. Meanwhile, the grunion hunters are scooping up all they can grab. They're trying to get as many of these squirming fish as possible into their containers.

A man looks at his watch. The time is 10:40 p.m. He wonders if some more grunion will come in with the next wave. Sometimes they do. Not a bad catch, he thinks, and starts to cook the fish over a driftwood fire.

The grunion have a very special clock inside them. They know that their eggs have the best chance of surviving if they don't get washed away by waves after they've been dug into the sand. So they wait until the tide is as high as it's going to get. They wait about fifteen minutes after the highest tide has passed, and then come ashore. Then they disappear back into the ocean and wait for the next highest tide, usually about two weeks later. During these two weeks, the eggs develop into fully formed fish. When the next high tide comes, these new grunion get washed into the ocean.

The Rhythms Around You

There are hundreds of examples of rhythms around you all the time. These are the changes that happen but with some regular pattern. They occur in repeating cycles you can observe over and over again. The examples you've read so far are good starters. But it's time for you to start noticing natural rhythms in the world yourself. You've probably noticed lots of them, but maybe you just haven't taken a good look yet. Here's a list of some to get you thinking.

1. The world changes in a constant rhythm of light to dark to light again. That's the cycle of a day.

2. The earth circles around the sun again and again. Each time it makes the round trip, the cycle of a year has been repeated. You can notice this by the seasons.

3. The moon revolves around the earth. You can see its cycle from new moon to full moon and back to new moon. This takes less than a month and is called the lunar cycle. Check page 67 for an idea about how to observe this.

4. The tides of the ocean go from high to low to high regularly. You can see this at the seashore. That tidal cycle takes just over twelve hours.

5. You have a rhythm of sleeping and waking and going to sleep again. Your cycle takes just about a day every time.

6. Trees and flowers start to bud on a yearly cycle that starts in the spring. Are there special trees or flowers nearby that give you a hint spring is coming, even when it's still wintery out?

7. Birds fly south at the same time every year. That's another annual rhythm. Have you ever noticed that the birds seem to get noisier at a certain time of the year? That's another signal that the weather is warming up.

8. There's a time of the year when flies and mosquitos get to be awful pests. This happens just about the same time every year. Do you know when that is? Try to notice next time.

9. Do you have pets? Have you noticed their regular cycles of sleeping and waking or of wanting to eat or go outside? If you've got tropical fish, check their colors in the daytime and at night.

How many of these rhythms had you noticed before reading about them? How may others can you add to the list right now? Tuck this idea of rhythms in your head, right behind your eyes, and see what you turn up as you're out looking into the world.

People-Made Rhythms

Some of the easier rhythms to spot out in the world aren't natural rhythms. Not only the natural world is so full of rhythms; people have used rhythms and cycles in lots of things they've done for many, many years. These may be easier for you to notice at first.

1. TRAFFIC LIGHTS AT INTERSECTIONS CHANGE IN REGULAR CYCLES THAT HAPPEN OVER AND OVER AGAIN.

2. WHEN A DRIVER PUTS ON THE DIRECTIONAL SIGNAL IN A CAR, THE LIGHT FLASHES ON AND OFF IN A REGULAR RHYTHM.

3. WINDSHIELD WIPERS HAVE A RHYTHM.

4. A RINGING TELEPHONE HAS A REPEATING RHYTHM OF RINGS.

5. CLOCKS AND WATCHES TICK WITH A REGULAR PATTERN.

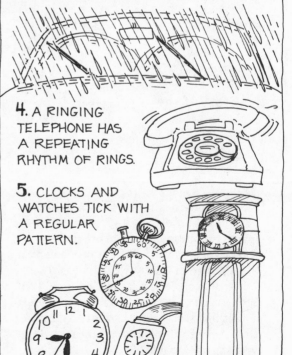

6. IN SOME SCHOOLS, BELLS RING EVERY DAY IN A REGULAR CYCLE. (DO THEY RING ON WEEKENDS TOO?)

7. THERE ARE REPEATING RHYTHMS IN MUSIC. YOU CAN HEAR AND FEEL THESE. SOMETIMES THIS IS CALLED "THE BEAT."

8. A LEAKY FAUCET WILL DRIP IN A REGULAR RHYTHM, WHETHER OR NOT YOU WANT IT TO.

9. THE WORLD SERIES HAPPENS EVERY YEAR. BASEBALL FANS KNOW WHAT TIME OF YEAR IT IS WHEN THAT EVENT COMES AROUND.

Start adding to this list. Check at home, in school, in stores, blinking advertisements on billboards, regular breaks on the radio, cycles of TV announcements. See if you can find at least five more things that have regular cycles to add to the list. The list is really endless. There's something so powerful about rhythms that they're impossible to ignore, once you start noticing.

The Big Question

Scientists have gotten interested in doing more than just observing rhythms and cycles in the world. Many have made careful investigations with plants and animals, trying to understand the secrets of biological rhythms. They've learned many things, but they haven't learned all there is to know.

There's one big question that these scientists have all wondered about. The question is: Are the natural rhythms in plants and animals *exogenous* rhythms or are they *endogenous* rhythms? Those two fancy words may be new to you, but if you're interested in learning about being a clockwatcher in the natural world, they're useful words to know about.

Exogenous rhythms happen because there is some external force that influences them. Endogenous rhythms happen because there is something inside the living organism that keeps this time, independent of any outside forces.

Scientists have done many experiments trying to answer the big question. Different theories have been suggested, but the scientists don't all agree. The reports that follow tell about some of the experiments scientists have done and what they've found. They'll help you to understand these two ideas.

Winter Clocks

Snowshoe rabbits have been used for some of the scientists' experiments. The snowshoe rabbit grows a white winter coat for protection against being seen in the snow. So do the weasel and the arctic fox. They all start changing their coats in late summer, and the change to white is complete by fall. How do these animals know when to start growing their winter coat so the camouflage is ready for the first snowfall?

84

This is what the scientists wondered about, so they did some experiments. They put snowshoe rabbits in a laboratory where they could be observed. They did this in early summer, before the coats of the rabbits started to change. The scientists wanted to see if they could get the rabbits to change the color of their coats sooner.

First they fiddled with the temperature in the laboratory, making it colder, to see if the temperature was the clue that the rabbits used to sense winter was coming. Nothing happened.

Then they wondered if light was the clue. The days start getting noticeably shorter in late summer. (Have you ever noticed this?) So the scientists blind-folded the rabbits for several hours each day to make them think that the days were getting shorter. Sure enough, their coats changed from brown to white much more quickly.

The scientists' conclusion was that the amount of light was the determining thing. But there were still questions. How did the rabbits keep track of the amount of light each day to notice that the days were getting shorter? How do their inner clocks keep this time?

Plants Sleep Too

Jean-Jacques De Mairan was a French astronomer who noticed that his mimosa plant opened and closed its leaves in a daily rhythm. In 1729, he reported this to France's Royal Academy of Science. He stated that when he put the plant in a dark closet, the plant had no way of knowing when it was day or night. Still, it continued to open and close its leaves in a regular rhythm. It was as if the plant had a cycle of being asleep and awake that ran on some inner clock.

His explanation was that the plant was so sensitive that it was able to sense the sun without being exposed to it in any way. But Jean-Jacques De Mairan did no more experiments on this theory. He was much more interested in astronomy.

Thirty years later, Henri-Louis Duhamel decided to do his own experiments about whether a plant really closed up its leaves even when it didn't know if it was day or night. He wasn't convinced that De Mairan's results were true. He lived in Paris and knew of an old wine cave nearby. He decided that this cave would be a perfect place to run a test of his own. So one morning in August, 1758, he carried a plant that opened and closed its leaves daily into the wine cave. While he was carrying the plant into the cave, he was careless and jostled the plant. It instantly closed up, just as if it had been hit. He was annoyed with himself, but he left the plant there and decided to check it the next day.

At 10:00 the next morning, he went back to the cave. He lit his candle and found that the plant had totally unfolded its leaves, just as if it were in broad daylight. The plant continued its cycle of opening and closing for many more days, just as if it were outside.

Henri-Louis Duhamel wanted to be sure. He tried the experiment with another plant. This time he put the plant into a large leather trunk, covered the trunk with heavy blankets, and then put it into a closed closet. That way there was absolutely no chance for any light to sneak in. What happened? The plant still closed up to sleep at night and opened in the morning.

He tried changing the temperature to see if that would have any effect, but the plant still carried on as usual. His conclusion was that the plant was perfectly capable of keeping its own time. It had an endogenous rhythm.

A Century Passes

No more experiments were done until a century later. Then Augustin Pyramus De Candolle, a Swiss botanist, started to investigate this plant-sleep cycle. His first experiments proved what both the other two men had found. Then he tried something new.

He arranged six lamps so that they shone constantly on the plants. The plants had no way of telling when night came, but still the plants slept at nighttime by closing up their leaves and woke up in the morning and unfolded them. The only difference was that the plants slept and awoke on about a twenty-two-hour cycle instead of a twenty-four-hour cycle each day.

Then he tried one more experiment. He wondered what would happen if he scheduled the lamps so the plants would be in light when it was really night outside and put into darkness when it was really daytime. He tried it. For a few days, the plants seemed very confused. But then they just readjusted, and soon they were sleeping and waking up on the schedule of the lamps. This was the exact reverse of the real day and night. Candolle had reset the plants' inner clocks, but those clocks kept their usual regular time within their new cycle.

Plant research has continued since that time. More scientists got curious. Erwin Bunning is a botanist who did a lot of research about this. He proved what had been discovered before but with different kinds of tests. In 1936, he wrote about two important ideas that he felt he discovered from his research. These two ideas made quite a stir among scientists.

Here is Dr. Bunning's first idea: Plants have their own internal clocks that control their own daily rhythms, which are endogenous rhythms, controlled totally within the plant. It is possible to reset their clocks, just as Candolle did with his lamps and just as you can reset any of your own clocks or watches at home. But once a plant is reset, its own internal rhythm takes over and keeps going.

The second idea Erwin Bunning had was this: Plants use their own internal rhythms to keep track of time passing in the world outside. That's how they know when to bud or flower or when to drop their leaves.

Scientists thought this was just too far-fetched to believe. Imagine a plant having its own clock, they thought. That was just too crazy to think about. But after other research was done with birds and bees and other living things, Dr. Bunning's clock idea began to take hold. The idea doesn't seem crazy to scientists today, even though they haven't found out everything they'd like to know about how this time sense works.

Your Own Plant Clock

A prayer plant is a houseplant that acts like the plants in these experiments. It goes to sleep at night by closing up its leaves, and it unfolds them in the morning. This plant is part of the maranta family of plants. Check in a local nursery to see if you can buy a small one. Then you can try some of your own experiments, and you can observe the workings of an internal clock yourself.

Bees' Built-In Clocks

People have noticed that bees are excellent timekeepers. Dr. Auguste Forel was the first to report this in 1906. Dr. Forel lived in Switzerland. In good weather, he liked to eat his breakfast on the terrace near his garden, and what he liked to eat included fresh jams and jellies.

Soon he noticed that he wasn't the only one who liked those jams and jellies. Bees always seemed to be buzzing around trying to get a taste. Dr. Forel ate breakfast at the same time every day, and the bees reliably came on time too.

Even though they were a bit of a nuisance, Dr. Forel got interested in their behavior. On mornings when he ate inside, he would check the terrace. Sure enough, there would be the bees, hopefully buzzing about. This puzzled him. How could the bees keep such good time? At first he had thought it was the aroma of the fruit in the jams that attracted them. But how could they know what time to come when there was no jam or jelly out there?

A few years later, Dr. Hugo von Buttel-Reepen also noticed how bees kept time. He often took walks through nearby buckwheat fields because he enjoyed the buckwheat flowers. They have a wonderful aroma. He got used to hearing the bees buzzing while they were collecting the nectar from the blossoms.

He also noticed that in the middle of the morning, at about 10:00, the bees would all leave. That was understandable to Dr. von Buttel-Reepen. He knew that the buckwheat flowers stopped their flow of nectar at about that time. The buckwheat flowers' inner clocks didn't interest him as much as the bees'. How did they know exactly when to come collect the nectar the next day? They always seemed to be on time.

He had a theory. He guessed that the bees had an actual time sense, some internal clock they used. He even gave this idea of a time sense a word in German, *zeitgedachtnis*. But is this time sense something that bees have within them, or is it controlled by some force out in the world?

A Complete Clock Check

Karl von Frisch studied the behavior of bees for many, many years. He wondered about the reports of their timekeeping, and in 1940, he designed an experiment to check on their inner clocks.

His idea was to train a group of bees to come for food at the same time every day, just like Dr. Forel had accidently done with his jams and jellies. Then he would build a box to hold the bees and put them on a fast boat to the United States. Would they keep feeding at local German time? If so, that would indicate they had independent internal clocks. Or would they shift their feeding time as they crossed time zones? This would show that they responded to outside clues.

Karl von Frisch built the rooms for the bees. He got an enthusiastic student to take the voyage with them and to note what time they came to feed each day. The student and the bees set out to sea.

Dr. von Frisch waited as patiently as he possibly could for the student to return with the reports, but not one single note had been made during the voyage. The student had been seasick the entire time and was never able to get out of bed.

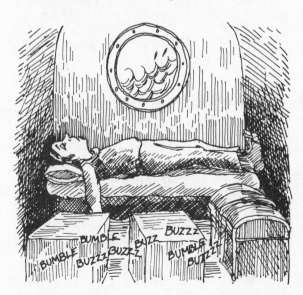

It wasn't until 1955 that Dr. von Frisch designed an experiment like that again. At this time there were lots of fast trans-atlantic flights to the United States, so there was no danger of seasickness. He asked his colleague, Max Renner, to take care of most of the details of this experiment.

Two bee rooms were built for the experiment. One was put together in Paris, and the other in the Museum of Natural History in New York. The rooms were eight by fifteen feet, and they were identical in every way.

In June, 1955, in Paris, Max Renner trained forty bees to come to a feeding dish between 8:15 and 10:15 in the morning according to local Paris time. When he decided they were all well trained, he packed them in a special box and flew with them to New York. When he got to New York, he raced to the Museum. In less than twenty-four hours after he had left Paris, the bees were in the other identical room.

Max Renner wondered if they would feed twenty-four hours after they had fed in Paris, or if they would feed at some new time since New York was on eastern standard/daylight saving time. What do you think happened? Max Renner sat near the feeding dish and waited for the answer. But he didn't have to wait long. Sure enough, twenty-four hours after they had fed in Paris, the first bees came out of the hive, just as if they were in Paris. It was 3:15 in the afternoon in New York.

This was an exciting answer to the question that Dr. Forel had wondered about fifty years earlier. The conclusion was that bees do have internal clocks that seem to be unaffected by the outside world. Dr. von Frisch felt that this timing ability of bees is an example of an endogenous rhythm. Check page 84 if you missed reading about what that word means.

Flowers That Bloom on Time

Carolus Linnaeus was a Swedish naturalist who designed a flower clock. He knew that certain flowers open and close at different times during the day. And he knew that they were reliable timekeepers, following their schedules to within half an hour on a sunny day. These flower clocks were often found in nineteenth-century European formal gardens.

You could try planting one yourself. Or you could just plant one or two of the flowers to see how they do as timekeepers when they're in bloom. Take this book to a nursery with you, and see which of the flowers you can find seeds or seedlings for. Ask the person in the nursery for some hints about how to care for these plants.

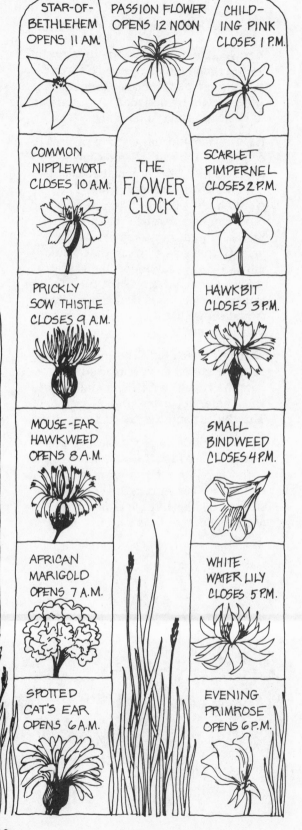

STAR-OF-BETHLEHEM OPENS 11 A.M.

PASSION FLOWER OPENS 12 NOON

CHILDING PINK CLOSES 1 P.M.

COMMON NIPPLEWORT CLOSES 10 A.M.

THE FLOWER CLOCK

SCARLET PIMPERNEL CLOSES 2 P.M.

PRICKLY SOW THISTLE CLOSES 9 A.M.

HAWKBIT CLOSES 3 P.M.

MOUSE-EAR HAWKWEED OPENS 8 A.M.

SMALL BINDWEED CLOSES 4 P.M.

AFRICAN MARIGOLD OPENS 7 A.M.

WHITE WATER LILY CLOSES 5 P.M.

SPOTTED CAT'S EAR OPENS 6 A.M.

EVENING PRIMROSE OPENS 6 P.M.

The Cycles of the Fiddler Crab

The fiddler crab is another well-timed creature. You can observe its time sense by the color of its shell. In the daytime, the fiddler crab has a dark greenish brown shell. In the nighttime, its shell is much lighter, a pale brown color. The change happens by spots of dark pigment in the shell that start to cluster together about the time of sunrise. This change from light to dark happens on a regular daily schedule of exactly twenty-four hours.

Not only does the fiddler crab's color follow this twenty-four-hour cycle daily, it pays attention to the tides as well. The time in the day when the fiddler crab's color is the darkest is always when the tide is lowest. That's when the crab is the most active, too, feeding on algae and other microorganisms left on the mud when the tide goes out. So the crab's dark shell at this time is a handy camouflage.

Low tide doesn't happen at the same time every day, though. Each day, low tide occurs about fifty minutes later than it did the day before. So each day, the crab's shell will be at its darkest fifty minutes later than it had been the day before.

The conclusion of biologists was that the crab has two internal clocks that are synchronized with each other. One is a rhythm that is tuned to tidal changes; the other is a twenty-four hour daily rhythm. The timekeeping ability of the fiddler crab has fascinated many scientists.

Is Internal Time Really Internal?

Dr. Frank A. Brown, Jr. is the scientist who did most of the investigations on the fiddler crab. He has done a great deal of other research in the area of biological rhythms too. And he's the most controversial scientist in his field today. That's because lots of what he believes seems to be just the opposite of what other scientists believe. The arguments have been fierce ones.

Dr. Frank Brown thinks that animals or plants do not have internal rhythms which operate independently from the forces in the world. He believes that there are cosmic forces in the universe that rule all living things. The moon's cycles, the force of gravity, the earth's motions are some examples of these cosmic forces. But there are others as well that are invisible, that you can't see or feel so easily, like electromagnetic waves or atmospheric rhythms. So even though animals seem to have endogenous internal clocks that run no matter what, these clocks are probably responding to some cosmic stimulus.

Here's an experiment Dr. Brown did that helped him come to his own conclusion. His question was: If you took a tidal creature that's timed according to the moon, like the fiddler crab, and transported it away from its home beach to a place where the tides were timed differently, what would happen? Would the animal stay on the rhythm of its home beach or would its cycles shift? What do you think would be the result?

Dr. Brown decided to find out, but instead of using the fiddler crab, which scurries around a lot on the beach, he chose an oyster. It doesn't have feet, can't move quickly, so it would be more convenient to observe.

Oysters were collected from the New Haven harbor in Connecticut and shipped to Illinois. They were kept in pans of sea water in a dark room. Right after they arrived, Dr. Brown observed that they continued to open their shells widest when it was high tide in New Haven, just as if they hadn't been moved at all.

But by the end of two weeks, they had totally reset their rhythms. Now they were opening their shells widest at the time when high tide would occur in Illinois, if Illinois were on the coast. They kept this new cycle for the entire month they were observed.

Frank Brown has continued his studies, investigating other animals and plants, even the potato. Though he hasn't discovered all he wants to, he's convinced that there are no purely internal rhythms. He believes that all living things respond to external stimuli and therefore have exogenous rhythms which scientists have just begun to explore.

How do you think Dr. Brown would explain the experiment with the plants that sleep and the bees that flew to New York? There's still much to learn.

Chapter 8
The Inside Story on People Time

You have your own inner clocks. They do the inside job of timing what goes on in your body. They're not like the clocks that help you time your activities during the day. Those clocks are out where you can easily see them — on walls, on wrists, sitting on table tops. Those timekeepers sometimes need your attention for winding or resetting.

But your inner clocks aren't visible to you. They don't need to be wound. You don't have to check them to see how time is moving. They do their job, day in and day out, automatically, with no help needed from you.

Inner clocks are what keep your biological rhythms well timed. They keep the inside parts of your body working together and timed with the outside world too. Do you know what some of your biological rhythms are?

Scientists have the same questions about human biological rhythms that they've had about the inner clocks of plants and animals. Even though your rhythms aren't as noticeable as plant and animal rhythms, they're there. And you can learn a great deal about them.

This section has information on what people have found out about human cycles. There are also activities and experiments, so you can try out some of what scientists have learned firsthand. Here's a chance for you to take a look at your own inner timing.

The Clock in You

How is your own sense of time? Take a quick check. Try guessing what time you think it is right now. Don't look at a clock yet. First make your guess as accurate as you think you can. Now go and check the clock. How close were you?

Investigate the time sense of some other people in your family. Try asking them what time they think it is. Do this on and off during the next several days. See how close their guesses are.

Some people set an alarm clock at night to be sure they'll get up in the morning by a certain time. Do you? Lots of people have reported that they always seem to wake up just before the alarm goes off. Has this ever happened to you? Has it happened to people you know? Ask your parents. Check with other people who use alarm clocks; see if this is generally true or untrue for them. If it's true for them, ask how come they still keep on setting the alarm at night?

Do you have a dog or a cat? If you do, try to observe their time sense. Some people notice that their pets seem to ask to be fed just about the same time every day. If you have a pet, check the times it shows up around the kitchen sniffing for some supper.

Not everyone's inner timing works with the same accuracy. Maybe you could improve your time sense. Try guessing the time on and off during the day whenever you remember. See if you can get more accurate. Do you think it's possible to sharpen your inner timekeeping?

The Man Who Was as Regular as Clockwork

A newspaper in England in the late 1880s reported that a man in a small village used to count out the chimes to tell the time when the village clock struck each hour. When the clock broke, he could still call out the hours at the right time. Do you know anyone who is as regular as clockwork?

People's Pacemakers

Some scientists feel that there is a pacemaker in everyone's brain that gives people some sense of time. Scientists don't know too much about this pacemaker. They do know that it's not a very trustworthy or accurate timekeeper for most people. They also know that humans don't do nearly as well as plants and animals do in keeping track of time. Maybe that's why people have spent so much of their energy inventing clocks to keep the time for them.

Scientists know that people's timing abilities are easily thrown off by changes. Heat is one of those changes. Have you ever had the feeling on a hot, hot day that time seems to be moving very slowly? Heat speeds up your pacemaker so your own sense of time is moving faster than time really is. Then things seem to take longer, as if they're happening in slow motion.

When you've got the flu or some nasty sickness that gives you a fever, the fever will have the same effect. Being sick in bed for a day with a fever often makes a day feel very long and slow.

When Frank Brown investigated the fiddler crab, heat changes had no effect whatsoever on the crab's daily color changes. When Henri-Louis Duhamel experimented with the plants that opened and closed their leaves on a daily cycle, temperature changes didn't change the plants' cycles at all. Your inner clocks just aren't that reliable.

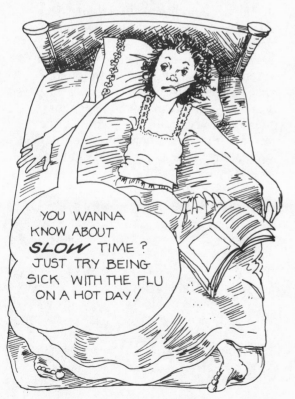

Are You an On-Time Person?

Are you a punctual person? Are you usually an early arriver, or are you a late comer? Most people fit clearly into one of those three timely groups. What about you?

Here are some questions to ask yourself if you're not sure which you are. When your mom or dad tells you to be home at 5:00 p.m., do you get home on time? Is it a struggle to do so, racing at the last minute to get there, or is it something you just plan for, so it's no big hassle?

Do you get ready to leave for school on time in the morning easily, or do you depend on someone else to keep you moving? Are you the one who always has to wait for someone else to finish getting ready?

What about the other people you live with or your friends? Predict whether you think they are on-timers, early arrivers, or late comers. Then ask them what they think, and see if your opinions agree.

How Late Is Late?

Some people think that arriving five minutes after an agreed-on time isn't really being late. Some people think that maybe ten minutes off would be late. Others think twenty minutes or half an hour can pass before someone would be too late. What do you think?

The Human Rhythms

One thing scientists have learned from their experiments to investigate human biological cycles is this: Many of your body rhythms operate on a twenty-four-hour cycle. These are daily rhythms. They operate automatically, without any effort from you.

These daily body rhythms are called circadian rhythms. The word *circadian* comes from two Latin words. *Circa* means "about" and *dies* means "day." Here's a listing of some of the circadian rhythms that are part of your everyday life.

1. *Your sleep-awake cycle.* This is an easy cycle for you to notice. Your brain controls your sleep-awake rhythm, and some of your other circadian rhythms are keyed to this one.

2. *Your body-temperature cycle.* Your temperature is regulated by the part of your brain called the hypothalamus. During a twenty-four-hour period, your temperature rises and falls about 1½ to 2 degrees Fahrenheit. It's lowest when you're asleep. And for most people, it's highest in the late afternoon.

Do you ever notice that when you're up watching a late movie on TV, you get really cold and need to huddle under a blanket? That's because your temperature is dropping for the night.

3. *Your oxygen-use rhythm.* Your cells need oxygen. How much oxygen they require varies in a daily cycle. When you run or exercise a lot, you breathe harder because your cells need more oxygen then. During the time of day that you're usually most active, your body's oxygen consumption is higher. When is this time of day for you? What's interesting is that even when you're not so active on some days, your rhythm of oxygen increase continues.

4. *The rhythm of your heartbeats.* The rate of your heartbeats changes on a daily cycle. When you're asleep, your heart beats slowest. Scientists have measured people's pulses and have found that they're usually lowest between 10 p.m. and 7 a.m. During the day, your pulse will vary according to how active you are. But even when you're resting or napping in the daytime, it won't be as low as it is at night.

5. *Your kidney-excretion cycle.* Your kidneys filter out the waste products from your blood. It expells these waste products in your urine. Your kidneys do most of this work during the day and less of it at night, when you're asleep. That's convenient, so you usually don't have to get up during the night to urinate.

6. *Your taste, smell, and hearing rhythms.* For most people, the sense of taste and smell and hearing are sharpest in late afternoon or evening. That's when people seem to be more aware of how good the dinner that's cooking smells, and how good it is to sit down and eat a yummy meal, and how sounds seem so much clearer or louder. Have you ever noticed any of these for yourself?

There are other body rhythms that scientists have discovered too. The ones listed are the ones you can observe most easily in yourself and in the people around you. Later in this chapter some experiments will help you take a closer look at your own cycles.

A Reminder About Rhythms

It's important to remember that people's individual cycles aren't all exactly the same. Living in a family where people's rhythms aren't all tuned in together makes for differences. Talk about these human rhythms with the other people in your family. Maybe you can get them interested in trying some of the activities that follow. That may give all of you another way to understand your differences and similarities.

Your Sleeping-Awake Cycle

Everyone needs to sleep. That's a biological law. When you sleep, your body gets a chance to restore the energy you've used up. When you don't have enough sleep, you act tired, you can't keep your attention on things well, you can't react as fast as you normally can, and you get generally grumpy.

How many hours do you sleep daily? Figure this out. If you're not sure, keep a record for a week. You can do that by making a chart like this and writing down the time you go to bed every night and when you get up every morning.

	WENT TO BED	GOT UP	HOURS
MONDAY			
TUESDAY			
WEDNESDAY			
THURSDAY			
FRIDAY			
SATURDAY			
SUNDAY			

Do you get up a different time on days that you don't have to go to school? Does that change how much sleep you get?

Kings Need to Sleep Too

Not everyone has believed that sleep is necessary. Napolean I, emperor of France, and Frederick the Great, king of Prussia, were two of these people. Even though they were leaders of their different countries at different times, they had one thing in common. They both thought sleep was just a bad habit that wasted time, and they both tried to prove it. They didn't do this together, but they both had the same method — staying up. But neither one lasted more than two nights, and they both needed several days to recover from their experiment.

Sleeping Ages with Time

The amount of sleep people need varies for individuals, but experiments have shown that age makes a big difference too. When you were a newborn baby, you slept on and off all during the day and night. You were asleep twice as much as you were awake, which meant you were sleeping about sixteen hours a day.

As you grow older, you need less and less sleep. Up until the time you are a teenager, you may sleep an average of about ten hours every night.

Grownups don't all need the same amount of sleep, but on an average, adults are awake twice as long as they are asleep. That means they sleep about eight hours out of every day. When grownups get older, they need even less sleep than that. People who are over sixty years old usually need only five to six hours.

Check these sleep times with people you know — friends, parents, grandparents, other relatives. See if the information you find agrees with what the experts have learned.

Sleepy Statistics

People spend about 33 percent of their lives asleep. Cows spend only 3 percent of their lives sleeping. Maybe that's because they have four stomachs, and they've got to spend a lot more time chewing than humans do.

Horses sleep just a little less of their lives than humans do, about 29 percent. But gorillas are asleep 70 percent of the time.

There Are Different Kinds of Sleep

Scientists have also discovered that there are cycles you go through as you sleep. You plunge down into deep sleep, up to lighter sleep, and down again to deep sleep. This happens all the time you're sleeping, in cycles that last about an hour and a half each. Scientists have learned this from studying people's brain waves while they're asleep. Here's the difference in how brain waves look when you're awake and when you're asleep, including different stages. Scientists have also learned that you do your dreaming when you're in the light-sleep stage.

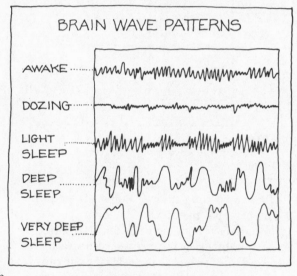

BRAIN WAVE PATTERNS

AWAKE

DOZING

LIGHT SLEEP

DEEP SLEEP

VERY DEEP SLEEP

WHAT DO YOU THINK TIME IS LIKE IN A DREAM? DOES ONE OF YOUR DREAMS TAKE ALL NIGHT OR ONLY A MOMENT?

Two-Timing

Here's a way to take a look at two of your daily cycles — your temperature cycle and your heartbeat cycle. The best time to do this experiment is on a day when you're not in school, so you can keep a record all through the day at regular times.

Get ready the night before you'll be doing the experiment. First make a recording chart, like the one shown. A piece of notebook-size paper will do fine. Notice that the chart is marked off every two hours. You'll start recording on your chart at the time listed that is closest to when you get up. Then take measurements at the other times listed during the day, stopping when you go to bed at night. Notice the space for answering the ten follow-up questions. You'll do that after you've taken all your statistics for the day.

| DATE _____ | | | FOLLOW-UP QUESTIONS |
TIME	TEMPERATURE	PULSE	
6 AM			1.
8 AM			2.
10 AM			3.
12 NOON			4.
2 PM			5.
4 PM			6.
6 PM			7.
8 PM			8.
10 PM			9.
			10.

The next thing to do is collect the equipment you'll need. You'll need a thermometer for taking your temperature, a thumbtack, a short piece of a straw — an inch or less — for taking your pulse. You'll also need a clock or watch with a second hand to time both your temperature taking and your pulse.

It's a good idea to practice taking both of these measurements once just to make sure you know how to do it. Here's how.

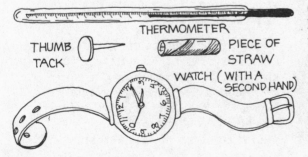

THERMOMETER

THUMB TACK

PIECE OF STRAW

WATCH (WITH A SECOND HAND)

Taking Your Temperature

1. CLEAN THE THERMOMETER. USE SOAPY WATER OR ALCOHOL. RINSE WELL.

2. SHAKE THE THERMOMETER DOWN UNTIL IT READS LESS THAN 96 DEGREES.

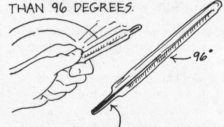

← 96°

3. PUT THE BULB UNDER YOUR TONGUE. IT NEEDS TO STAY THERE FOR A GOOD THREE MINUTES, SO TIME THAT WITH THE CLOCK OR WATCH. (NOTICE HOW LONG THREE MINUTES SEEMS LIKE TOO.)

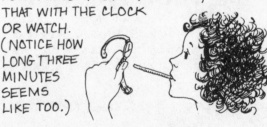

4. READ YOUR TEMPERATURE.

5. CLEAN THE THERMOMETER BEFORE PUTTING IT AWAY.

Check with your parents for a quickie lesson about how to take your temperature and read the thermometer, if you're not sure. The average human body temperature is 98.6 degrees Fahrenheit, but not everyone has exactly that temperature normally. Don't be concerned if yours is a degree or two above or below this figure.

Taking Your Pulse

1. PUT THE PIECE OF STRAW ON THE POINT OF THE THUMBTACK.

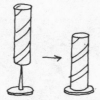

2. PLACE ONE HAND, PALM UP, ON A TABLE TOP.

3. PUT THE STRAW-THUMB TACK APPARATUS ON YOUR WRIST, ON THE OUTSIDE EDGE. MOVE IT ABOUT UNTIL YOU FIND THE SPOT WHERE YOUR PULSE IS THE STRONGEST. YOU CAN TELL BECAUSE THE STRAW MOVES MORE.

4. COUNT EACH TIME THE STRAW MOVES UP. DO THIS FOR FIFTEEN SECONDS.

5. MULTIPLY THE NUMBER YOU COUNTED BY FOUR. THIS WILL GIVE YOU THE NUMBER OF TIMES YOUR HEART BEATS IN ONE MINUTE.

If you know another way to take your pulse, that's fine too. When you do the experiment, take your temperature readings and pulse counts carefully all through the day. When you've got your chart completed, see how your information measures up to these follow-up questions.

What Does Your Chart Show?

1. What's the lowest temperature you recorded all day?

2. What's the highest temperature?

3. How big a difference is there between these two readings?

4. At what time was the highest reading?

5. When was your temperature the lowest?

6. What was the slowest pulse reading you took?

7. What was the fastest pulse measurement?

8. When was your pulse the fastest?

9. When was it the slowest?

10. Can you see any relationship between when your pulse was fastest and when your temperature was highest?

According to scientists, your temperature should have been highest late in the afternoon or in the evening, and lowest in the early morning. Does your cycle agree with this? Also scientists say that most people have a 1½ to 2 degree variation all day. Was this true for you? Your pulse should have been lowest when you first got up, according to scientists. It should be highest at your usual time of greatest activity.

A Statistical Caution

Remember, scientists did many, many tests before they came up with their conclusions. What you've done is just one sample of your daily cycle of temperature and pulse changes. Not only can your cycles differ somewhat from what the reported averages are, your own rhythms can change a bit from day to day. You've got a lifetime to spend with your body rhythms. Trying the experiment on another day will give you a chance to take another look.

Ears Tell Time Too

For some people, loud noises become very annoying when their hearing sense is sharpest. This is usually in the late afternoon or early evening. Do you ever notice during those times that your parents seem to tell you that you're being much too noisy or that the TV is too loud? Then at other times during the day, the same noise doesn't seem to bother them so much. Maybe it's because they're extra weary at the end of a long workday. But it's also the time of day when most people's hearing is most sensitive.

If this seems to check out with your parents, maybe you could explain it to them. You could say: "You're annoyed because the circadian rhythm of your senses is at its highest now." But say it softly, and then maybe you'd just better be a bit quieter anyway.

P. S. If they ask you what a circadian rhythm is, could you answer them? Remember, a circadian rhythm is one that occurs in a daily cycle. It runs on a twenty-four-hour clock.

Are You a Day Person or a Night Person?

What time of day do you feel you have the most energy to do things, think clearly, or tackle problems? Do you think it's during the day or at night? You're a day person if the daytime is when you function best, and you're a night person if the night is your best time. If you're not sure which you are, ask yourself these questions to help you decide. Jot down yes or no for each one.

1. At night, do you get sleepy easily, even when you thought you'd love to stay up and watch that movie on TV?

2. Are you often wide-awake when your parents tell you that they don't care if there's no school tomorrow, just get yourself to bed and now?

3. Do you bounce out of bed all cheery and wide-awake in the morning?

4. Are you the kind of person that would just as soon have no one talk to you when you get up in the morning until you are good and ready?

5. If you have a homework assignment to do and it's late at night, would you rather go to bed and get up early in the morning to do it?

6. When night comes, do you still have lots of energy to do stuff?

Day people would most likely answer yes on the odd-numbered questions. Night people probably would say yes to the even ones. Does this help you decide which you are?

Try a poll of others to see how the people you know sort out into day people or night people. Your inner clocks do affect how you act and feel. Remember that not everyone's clocks are set exactly the same. The more you know about your own rhythms, the more you can understand how you react at different times.

Do You Have Day Pets or Night Pets?

Just like people can be sorted into day people and night people, so can pets. Dogs and birds are generally thought to be day pets. They're called diurnal. But cats and hamsters are nocturnal. When night comes, they get more active. Do you have any pets? Are they day pets or night pets?

Do you think that more day people have day pets than night pets or that night people usually have night pets? Make a list of the people you know who have pets. The best list to make would be of the people who actually made the choice for that particular pet, not just someone in a family where there's a dog or a cat. Then check out if those people are day or night people and see if that matches up with their pets at all. What do you think might be the results of this experiment?

One caution: Don't call any people you think are night people too early in the morning. They might be awfully grumpy.

Can You Kick the Twenty-Four-Hour Habit?

Nathaniel Kleitman and Bruce Richardson tried to kick the twenty-four-hour habit. These two men wondered if it would matter much to people if the day were longer, so, in 1938, they decided to try and find out.

They knew that people have a daily twenty-four-hour cycle of waking and sleeping. They also knew that newborn babies don't seem to give a hoot about a twenty-four-hour day. Babies' clocks are their stomachs; they sleep and eat on and off all during the day and night. If you have a younger sister or brother, you may know this firsthand or you may know it from hearing your parents wonder when the baby was ever going to sleep through the night without being fed. But babies eventually learn to adjust to the twenty-four-hour day.

Nathaniel Kleitman and Bruce Richardson thought about this and wondered if a person could learn to live on a longer daily cycle. They decided to experiment on themselves to see if they could learn to do it. What they did was shut themselves up in Mammoth Cave, Kentucky, where they couldn't tell whether it was day or night outside. They did this for thirty-two days, staying in a chamber that was sixty by twenty feet. They decided to put themselves on a twenty-eight-hour schedule per day by staying awake for nineteen hours and sleeping for nine hours.

Bruce Richardson had no trouble. Within a week, a twenty-eight-hour day seemed fine to him and to his body too. His temperature changes just readjusted to the new cycle with highs when he was awake and lows when he slept. All his other rhythms fell into step too.

Not so for Nathaniel Kleitman. His body was just plain stubborn, sticking to the normal twenty-four-hour daily cycle it was used to. He was often sleepy and grumpy during their waking hours and restless when they were trying to sleep.

There was one difference between the two men that they figured was the reason for this. Bruce Richardson was twenty years younger. Resetting Nathaniel Kleitman's inner clockworks may have been more difficult for him since it had twenty extra years of practice on the twenty-four-hour cycle. Do you think this might have been the reason, or do you have another idea?

An Experiment in Stretching and Shrinking the Day

In the 1950s, Dr. Mary Lobban organized an experiment that was done in northern Norway. It was done during the time of the year when that part of Norway is in constant sunlight. Check page 28 if you'd like to know more about how it's possible for part of the world to be in twenty-four-hour sunlight.

Here's how the experiment was organized. There were two groups of people. Each group lived in a different town and had no contact with the other group or with anyone else outside the group except for the scientist in charge.

The people in each group were given watches that were really "cheating" wrist watches. They had been specially adjusted. For one group, the watches were slowed down so that they actually took twenty-eight hours to tick off a normal day of twenty-four hours. For the other group, the watches were speeded up, so a day on their watches took only twenty hours. Both groups stayed in their villages for eight days. None of them knew about how their watches had been fiddled with.

People in both groups adjusted easily. None of them reported the discomfort that Nathaniel Kleitman had felt. Those who had the slowed-down watches actually believed that they had been there for nine days. The group with the speeded-up watches were sure they had been there for seven.

Letting Time Free-Run

What would happen if you tried an experiment like Nathaniel Kleitman and Bruce Richardson did or like Mary Lobban organized? Suppose you didn't take any watch with you. You'd have no idea what time it was, and you'd be shut off from all clues from the outside world. Scientists who study biological rhythms call this free-running.

Michel Siffre tried it. On July 16, 1962, he climbed down into a cave in the Alps. He had all he needed to stay underground, except a watch. Michel Siffre's only link with the outside world was a telephone. He used the telephone to tell the experimenters when he ate, went to sleep, or woke up. Whenever he gave this information, he recorded what time he thought it was, too. That way, when he came up from the cave, his record and the actual time record of the experimenters above could be compared.

Michel Siffre's own time records were completely wrong. By his figuring, he had been in the cave for thirty-six days. But actually, he'd been there for sixty-one days! He thought that he wasn't sleeping and waking on a twenty-four-hour cycle. He thought his cycle was much shorter — only fifteen hours. He was wrong. His actual cycle of eating and sleeping and waking up was a twenty-four-and-a-half-hour rhythm.

Can you imagine what it would be like to be alone in a cave for two months? Can you imagine what Michel Siffre's thoughts were when he first saw daylight after sixty-one days?

More Clock Setting

Some volunteers in Germany tried an experiment to see what would happen if they tried to set their own clocks, like Michel Siffre did. This was a much bigger experiment, though. There were 130 volunteers. They were shut inside, so they couldn't tell what was going on out in the world. They had no clocks or watches.

Most people wound up living on twenty-five- or twenty-six-hour days. One man shifted to a fifty-hour day. He'd work and read for thirty hours and sleep for twenty. They were all there for three weeks. He was convinced he had been there for ten days.

Living Your Own Time

Suppose you're a person who would live a twenty-six- or twenty-seven-hour day if you let your body give the orders instead of the sun or the kitchen clock or your mom. Suppose you decided to do it, to let your body free-run. How would that be, living in a twenty-four hour world?

You'd go to bed at night when you were tired. But each night that would be an hour or so later than you went to bed the night before, which means you'd get up later too. So if you went to bed at 10:00 one night and got up at 7:00 in the morning, the next night you might go to bed at 11:00 and sleep until 8:00. That wouldn't be too bad. But a week later, you'd be going to bed at 5:00 in the morning, and getting up in the early afternoon and staying up until 6:00 the following morning before sleeping again.

What problems would this cause? You'd hardly ever make it to school on time. You'd be up in the middle of the night when all your friends were sleeping. You'd miss lots of movies and TV shows you might want to see because you'd be asleep. You'd be ready for breakfast sometimes when the rest of the family was sitting down to dinner. How do you think this kind of life would be?

Living Clocks Are Still a Mystery

There are scientists who feel sure that human rhythms are closely connected to larger forces in the universe. They feel that somehow our cycles and the cycles in the rest of the natural world are all connected in ways people don't know too much about.

They feel that cracking the mystery of human cycles may make a big change in medical science. Some experiments have already been done in this area. There have been experiments showing that people who are sick respond to medication better at different times of the day. Investigations have been made showing that various diseases have their own observable rhythms. Studying biological rhythms may give doctors entirely new ways to cure illnesses.

There is lots to be learned. The big breakthrough in the theory of living clocks hasn't been made. Men and women will continue to study all they can for a long time.

Maybe you will too. How would you feel about making a career in biological rhythms your lifework? It would be an exciting choice and one that could benefit all of humanity.

Chapter 9
What Is Jet Lag?

Airplanes travel faster than human-body clocks can keep up. That causes a problem for people who fly long distances, and the problem is called jet lag.

Here's an example of jet lag. Suppose some people are in Tokyo, Japan, on a Tuesday. They eat lunch and then get on a plane to fly home to Los Angeles. During that trip, they cross seven time zones, plus the International Date Line. (Check Chapter 2 if you need to know what that's all about.) All these time zone changes take place in a flight that takes about nine hours. When the plane lands, their bodies feel like it's almost midnight. But in Los Angeles, it's 6:00 in the morning, still on Tuesday! It's actually earlier than when the plane left Tokyo.

If this story confuses you from just reading it, imagine how your body would feel if you were on that plane. You can reset your wrist watch, but you can't reset your body that easily. That's when jet lag hits.

The Jet-Lag Tests

The Federal Aviation Agency has done tests to learn more about what jet lag really does to people. The members of this agency are concerned with safe air flights for people. They wondered about the problem of flight crews getting jet lag.

Once, they did a series of three tests. In each test, the four-person flight crew was used for collecting information. For the first test, the crew on a flight from Oklahoma City to Manila, in the Philippines, was used. That trip took about ten hours and crossed nine time zones. After they arrived, the crew members were given some tests to do during the next day.

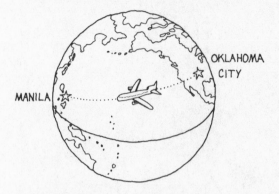

The third test was done on a crew that flew from Washington, D. C., to Santiago, Chile. No time zones were crossed, even though that flight took longer than the Rome flight. The crew had none of the problems that the other two crews had.

It turned out that for twenty-four hours after they arrived, none of them were able to concentrate long enough to add a column of ten, two-digit numbers. They tested their reaction times too. They did this by asking the crew members to press a button when a light was flashed. They had timed these reactions before the flight. The result was that now all of their reactions were greatly slowed down. Some of their reactions took three times as long as they normally did.

Another flight used went from Oklahoma City to Rome. This headed in the opposite direction. The flight crossed seven time zones. The four-person crew did no better on the tests afterwards than the crew on the Manila flight did.

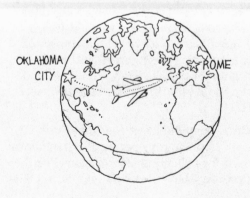

The conclusion seemed clear: Crossing all those time zones makes your body miserable. The Federal Aviation Agency used these results to set up rules for how much time flight crews should be allowed to work and how much rest they need before working again. You wouldn't want a pilot with a bad case of jet lag flying a plane full of trusting passengers.

The Jet-Lag Cure

There's only one known cure for jet lag. That's rest. Your body needs rest so it has a fair chance to readjust. It's possible to figure out about how much rest your body will need in order to catch up after a long trip. The International Civil Aviation Organization has a clever formula you can use.

You need to have four pieces of information to use the formula:
1. How much travel time will the flight take in hours?
2. How many time zones more than four will you cross?
3. What time will you leave?
4. What will the local time be where you arrive?

The two times in questions 3 and 4 need to be changed into two special numbers in the formula according to this table:

TIMES	DEPARTURE TIME NUMBER (CALL IT D)	ARRIVAL TIME NUMBER (CALL IT A)
8:00 AM – 11:59 AM	0	4
12:00 NOON – 5:59 PM	1	2
6:00 PM – 9:59 PM	3	0
10:00 PM – 12:59 AM	4	1
1:00 AM – 7:59 AM	3	3

And when you've got the four pieces of information you need, put them into this formula:

$$\frac{\text{TRAVEL TIME}}{2} + \text{TIME ZONES MORE THAN 4} + D + A$$

Then multiply the number you get from all that by 2.4. A calculator comes in handy here, or so does a grownup to help with the decimal multiplication, if you haven't learned that in school yet. The final answer will be the number of hours you'll need to rest to give your body a fair shake.

Here's a sample of how that formula works on a plane trip across the United States. There's a flight that leaves San Francisco at 9:00 a.m. and arrives in New York at 5:59 p.m. New York time.

The trip takes six hours and crosses three time zones. The time zones don't count in the formula since they're less than four. Here's how the figuring would go:

$$\frac{6}{2} + 0 \text{ TIME ZONES} + 0 + 2 = 5$$

And 5 multiplied by 2.4 gives 12 hours. That's half a day's rest that's needed after that trip.

A Jet-Lag Travelers' Service

Maybe you could start a jet-lag service for travelers. Keep your ears open to hear about people taking long trips. Then you could figure the time they'll need to rest when they arrive. They could even mail you a message from wherever they went to let you know how their bodies did.

What About Ship Lag?

Travel exhaustion wasn't a problem when people traveled by ship. In 1907, an English doctor sailed from Australia to London. He changed his watch whenever the clocks aboard ship were changed. That was done each time another time zone was crossed.

He felt fine during the trip. When he arrived in London, his daily temperature cycle was right where it was expected to be. His high temperature of the day was at 6:00 p.m. London time, even though that was 4:00 a.m. Australian time when he'd be fast asleep and cool as a cucumber. (Check Chapter 8 for why his temperature told him about his body.)

Around the World with Wiley Post

There is something you can do about jet lag if you get started far enough before a trip. You can try a kind of preventative medicine — that is to readjust your body clock before you go.

Wiley Post was a record-setting world flier in the 1930s. He did a lot of long-distance flying in Winnie Mae, his airplane. Even though that was before all the experiments were done about jet lag and before that fancy formula had been figured out, Wiley Post knew about the problem from experience.

He knew that when he crossed lots of time zones, his sleeping, his eating, and his general well-being wasn't so hot. So what he'd do before some of his long flights, which were seven or eight days of flying, was to practice irregular sleeping and eating to get his body used to different rhythms. He said it helped.

Persons planning a long trip can try to retrain their bodies before they go. If they know that there's a three-hour time difference flying from San Francisco to New York, then they can try staying up a little later each night for a few nights and getting up a little later too. That would help get their body used to New York time more gradually. No use going on a big vacation and being too tired when you get there to do anything.

If people can't do anything about resetting their inner clocks before going, then they'd better add the resting time into their plans on the other end. No use getting too grouchy after you arrive.

REMEMBER ABOUT JET LAG WHEN YOU HAVE A VISITOR WHO'S FLOWN A LONG WAY.

The Timely Tale of the Tired Texas Pelicans

About twenty years ago, three Texas pelicans were flown to London, England. That was because several of the pelicans that had lived in the gardens of Buckingham Palace had died, and these three pelicans were replacements.

When they arrived, the pelicans were first taken to the London Zoo. The head keeper of the zoo wasn't very impressed with them. "I have never seen such sleepyheads as these Texas pelicans," he said. What he said was broadcast on the radio all the way to the United States.

Dr. Hubertus Strughold was listening to the radio and heard this report. He was living in Texas and had studied the effects of space travel and air travel on people for a long time, so he knew a lot about jet lag.

Dr. Strughold wrote a letter to the head keeper explaining that for both pelicans and people, being a sleepyhead was expected after a flight that crossed seven time zones. He explained that the pelicans still had Texas time in them, and it would take a while for their bodies to adjust to Big Ben, the clock on the tower of the British Parliament.

Three weeks later, the zoo keeper wrote back. The pelicans were doing fine now. They were as friendly as pelicans are expected to be and ready to join the other animals in the palace gardens. Dr. Strughold not only taught the zoo keeper something about jet lag, he also saved the reputations of those three Texas pelicans.

Do Migrating Birds Get Jet Lag?

Some birds have both summer and winter homes. They make two long distance trips a year between them. That's called migrating. Do these birds get jet lag?

People who study birds are called ornithologists. They've studied this very question. They've learned that the two homes of most long-distance migrating birds aren't more than two or three time zones apart. This way the birds don't have to adjust to drastic changes.

There are some birds that are exceptions, however. The arctic tern is one of those. This bird spends summers in the Arctic and winters in the Antarctic. It travels between those two homes by way of Labrador, Iceland, Scotland, the Atlantic coast of France, and the western coast of Africa. Trace that route on a map or globe. The trip is more than ten thousand miles and crosses five time zones. But the arctic tern knows about the resting method for preventing jet lag. It stops to rest frequently on islands and coastlines.

Maybe there are some other things you could learn from birds, if you stopped to watch.

Chapter 10

Time in Your Life

Here's a last set of time exercises. They're designed to stretch your look at time just a bit further. This collection of activities will get you looking back in time, ahead to your future time, and out in the universe to interplanetary time. Take the time now to try these.

How Long Is Long Ago?

Most people would agree that Columbus set sail for the New World long ago. That was back in the fifteenth century. But how far back in time does something have to be to have happened "long ago"? Read through the list of events below. Note the first event you come to that you don't think happened long ago. That's probably a good estimate of when you think long ago stopped.

1. The first roller skates were invented in 1760. Was that long ago?

2. How about when the first long-distance pigeon race was held? That was in 1871. Do you think that was long ago?

3. The ice cream cone was invented in 1904. Was that long ago?

4. The New York Yankees won their first World Series in 1923. Was that long ago?

5. How about when the first Mickey Mouse watch was made. That was in 1934. Does that seem like long ago to you?

6. The person who wrote this book was born in 1941. Was that long ago?

7. In 1949, the song "Rudolph the Red-Nosed Reindeer" was recorded. Was this long ago?

8. Edmund Percival Hillary climbed to the top of Mt. Everest in 1953. Do you think that was long ago?

9. The movie "Around the World in Eighty Days" won the Academy Award for best picture in 1956. Was that long ago?

10. The Beatles became popular recording stars in 1963. Do you think that was long ago?

11. July 20, 1969, was the first time any person set foot on the moon. Was that long ago?

12. What about when you started first grade? Was that long ago?

When do you think long ago starts? Decide which year feels about right as a possible answer to that question. Show this list to other people and see when long ago starts for them. Ask one of your grandparents and see what they say. Ask your parents too. Ask other kids who are the same age as you are. See what you learn about what different-age people think long ago means.

How Many Days Old Are You?

How many days have you been living so far? People usually measure their ages by years, but that doesn't have to be the only way. Figure out how many days old you are today.

Here's a time tip: Don't forget about leap years. They come every fourth year and have an extra day. The years that are leap years are the ones that can be divided by four with no remainder. Here's a listing of some of the leap years to help you: 1984, 1980, 1976, 1972, 1968, 1964, 1960, and so on.

Next time you're planning to wish someone a happy birthday, why not design your own birthday card for them. It can say something like this: Congratulations for having been alive for 3,721 days! Keep up the good work! Imagine a birthday cake with a candle on it for each day instead of for each year. That would be some birthday blaze.

114

How Old Would You Be on Mars?

Your first birthday came after you had lived for one year. In that time, the earth made one complete revolution around the sun and returned to the position it was in when you were born. That's what a year is — the time it takes the earth to do this, going through all four seasons.

Now try this idea on your imagination. Suppose you went to visit Mercury when you were one year old. Just suppose there were people on Mercury just like earth people. They'd take a look at you and think you looked just like a four-year-old. If you went to Mars, however, you'd only look like you'd been around for about half a year. On Saturn, you'd need to live thirty earth years before you'd look like a one-year-old Saturn person

It's not that you'd look any different. You wouldn't go to school any earlier or be able to drive a car any sooner. Your biological age wouldn't change. But your chronological age would be calculated differently on each planet.

The reason for this is that the closer a planet is to the sun, the faster it travels, and it also has a shorter distance to go to travel once around the sun. So the planets that are nearer to the sun have shorter years, since it takes them less time to make a complete revolution.

The earth makes the trip around in about 365¼ days. Here's how long it takes the other planets to make their round trips, measured by earth time.

PLANET	LENGTH OF YEAR (EARTH TIME)
MERCURY	88 DAYS
VENUS	225 DAYS
EARTH	365.26 DAYS
MARS	687 DAYS
JUPITER	11.9 YEARS
SATURN	29.5 YEARS
URANUS	84 YEARS
NEPTUNE	164.8 YEARS
PLUTO	248.4 YEARS

If you are ten years old now, here's about what your age would be on each of the planets.

PLANET	AGE OF A TEN-YEAR-OLD
MERCURY	41.5 YEARS OLD
VENUS	16.2 YEARS OLD
EARTH	10 YEARS OLD
MARS	5.3 YEARS OLD
JUPITER	ABOUT 10 MONTHS OLD
SATURN	ABOUT 4 MONTHS OLD
URANUS	ABOUT 1.4 MONTHS OLD
NEPTUNE	ABOUT 3 WEEKS OLD
PLUTO	ABOUT 2 WEEKS OLD

This is a problem that's easiest to do with a hand calculator. Figure out how old you'd be now on any of the planets.

The First Time of Your Life

Some people believe that your life is tied to the rest of the universe from the time of your birth. They think that the positions that the sun, moon, stars, and planets were in when you were born is the key to understanding a lot about you. Not only is the day you were born important, but the time of day is too. What do you think about this? Do you know what time of day you were born?

The study of that belief is called astrology. It's been around for over five thousand years. Early astrologers studied the patterns of how the sun and moon and planets and stars moved. They learned to use that information to predict the seasons and eclipses, the changing phases of the moon, and the movements of the stars and planets. Some people think that the study of astrology was the beginning of the study of astronomy.

Then astrologers began to make other predictions about the world — about the futures of kingdoms and the outcomes of battles, big events like those. Then they began to predict the futures of individual people. After all, they figured, if the world seems to be ruled by the rhythms of the sun and moon and planets and stars, why wouldn't these forces affect all living things — people included.

The beliefs of astrology have never been proved, but they've never been disproved, either. Some people think astrology is all nonsense. Some people think it makes perfect sense. And some people aren't quite sure one way or the other.

Most newspapers print daily horoscopes. Check a newspaper if you've never looked for the horoscopes before. The horoscopes are organized by your sign of the zodiac. Do you know your sign?

Each sign's horoscope is given daily to predict what you can expect to happen that day.

What do the people you know think about astrology and horoscopes? Here's a way to find out. Ask as many people as you can these four questions and see what conclusions you can make.

1. Do you know what your sign of the zodiac is?

2. How often do you read your horoscope in the newspaper: never, sometimes, or regularly?

3. Do you take the predictions in your horoscope seriously, a little bit seriously, or do you read it just for fun?

4. Do you ever change your day's plans because of what you've read in your horoscope?

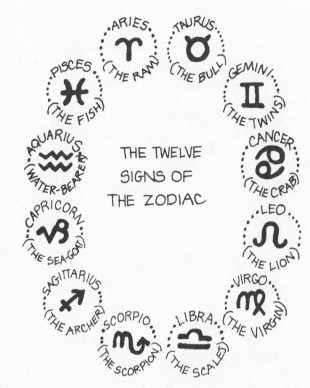

How Far Back Can You Remember?

Can you remember things that happened to you when you were much younger — things from the first grade or back before you went to school? Try fishing in your mind for some long-ago memories. When you've got one, ask yourself these questions about it:

1. HOW OLD DO YOU THINK YOU WERE THEN?

2. WHAT WERE YOU DOING?

3. CAN YOU REMEMBER HOW YOU FELT THEN?

4. CAN YOU REMEMBER WHAT OTHER PEOPLE WERE THERE, TOO, IF ANY?

If you can answer three of those four questions, jot those memories down. Then check later with your parents and see if they remember the same thing in the same way you do.

Ask your parents to tell you memories from their lives when they were your age or younger. Ask each one the same four questions. You may learn something about them you don't know yet.

A Strip on Time

Here's another way to take a look back. Cut a strip of paper about the size and shape of a twelve-inch ruler. This is your life-line strip. It represents all the time in your life so far. One end of the strip marks the time you were born. The other end is right now, the present time.

If you don't have your strip yet, make one now. Then put five marks on the strip. Each of the marks you make shows a special time of your life. These special times are listed. You have to place the marks where you think that time would go on your strip. Number each mark to fit the description given.

1. YESTERDAY.

2. LAST WEEK.

3. YOUR LAST BIRTHDAY.

4. FIVE YEARS AGO.

5. WHEN YOU WERE IN FIRST GRADE.

Do you think the other people in your family would mark their time strips just like you did? You can find out. Make a strip for each of the people in your family and give them the same instructions you followed. Then compare strips. It might be fun to mix up the strips after you've all made yours, and see if someone can guess who belongs to which one. If you've got a grandparent living near you, ask them to strip their lives too; that will make an interesting comparison.

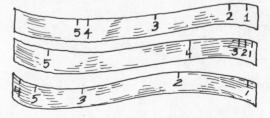

118

Can You See into the Past?

When you look at photographs of yourself when you were a baby, you're getting a peek at the past. Home movies do that, too, if you've got them. Those are two clear examples of looking back into the past.

Here's another example that might not be so clear. Whenever you look at a star, you are looking at the past. Why? Take Polaris, the North Star for starters. It is three hundred light-years away from earth. This means that it takes three hundred years for the North Star's light to get to where you are, so you're seeing Polaris the way it looked three hundred years ago.

It's possible to be looking at a star that doesn't even exist. Suppose a star is born that is one thousand light-years away from earth. By the time that star's light gets to earth so it can be seen, one thousand years have passed, and the star might have already died.

Out-of-Date

Do you have any things that are out-of-date? Do you know what out-of-date means? Ask your parents if you're not sure.

Some things go out-of-date for a while, and then they make a comeback. The Two-dollar bill is an example. These were first issued in August, 1862. In 1966, the federal government stopped printing them, and they pretty much disappeared. Then on April 13, 1976, the government started making them again. That was on Thomas Jefferson's birthday. His picture is on the bill. Have you seen many? Why do you think the Treasury Department decided to re-issue them? Do you think they will go out-of-date again?

Some songs go out-of-date pretty quickly. Can you think of any pop or rock songs that you once liked a lot but seem old and out-of-date now? If you can't, ask one of your parents to sing a song for you that they used to like a lot. Or else, play an old record that's been around the house for a while that no one listens to anymore. What makes it sound so out-of-date?

Make an out-of-date search around your house. Look around and see how many things you can find that you think will be out-of-date someday. Decide which things you think will never be out-of-date. Check kitchen appliances, clothing, furnishings, toys, and games. Put what you think into two lists and check with your parents to see if they agree.

What's the oldest thing in your house? Is it older than your grandparents? Are there any things in your house that could be called antiques? How old do you think something has to be, to be considered an antique? Check your parents' opinion on that. If you live near a store that sells antiques, you might ask the person who works there.

There are some people who wonder if the penny will ever be out-of-date. They say that things will cost so much someday, that there won't be any use for the penny at all. What do you think about this?

Growing Up with Time

Can you remember when you first learned how to tell time? Can you ever remember being told that you have half an hour more to play, and then it seemed like your time was up in only five minutes? Think back to when you were younger, and see if you can recall any thoughts about time. Check with your parents and see if they remember how old you were when you were able to tell your age to someone who asked or when you knew for sure which day was your birthday.

It takes a while for little kids to develop an understanding of time. Here's an experiment you can try on a child who is three or four years old. Ask them each of the five questions, in order. But before you do, try to predict what you think their answers will be.

1. Is your mom older or younger than you are?

2. Was she born before you or after you?

3. Who came first, your mom or you?

4. Do you always stay the same age, or do you grow older?

5. How about your mom? Does she always stay the same age, or does she grow older?

Try this with other kids if you can, different ages, too, and compare the answers you get.

The Year 2100

Suppose you were given the job of packing a box that wasn't going to be opened for over a hundred years — one century. You were told that in the year 2100, kids as old as you are now would open the box to see what was inside. This box was to be a time capsule that would tell them about kids' lives as they are now.

How big a box would you need? Would a shoe box be big enough, or would you need one as big as a refrigerator? (Would you want to put a refrigerator in your time capsule?) What things would be important to include?

What foods or sporting equipment or books and magazines? Check your ideas with a friend to see if they agree.

Would you really like to have that job? Maybe you could suggest it to your teacher as a class project.

What do you think your parents would have packed if they did it when they were your age? Make some predictions and then ask. You'll get a glimpse of what was important to them when they were kids.

Your Life Line

Here's a way to link the past, present and future times of your life and be able to take a look at them too. Follow these directions to make your own life line.

You'll need ten index cards, some colored markers, and yarn or string. These ten cards will tell the story of your life, and that includes the part of your life that hasn't even happened yet — your future.

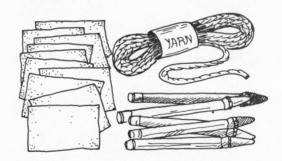

On each card, write one important event or happening or period in your life. Choose things like "I was born" or "I went to elementary school" or "I moved to a new place." Illustrate each card so the event gets pictured too. Since there are only ten cards, the events you pick should be ones you think are the most important milestones in your life.

Here are some more directions before you get started. Three of the cards are for your past — things that already have occurred. One of the cards should be about the present. That means you need to choose one thing in your present life that best describes what your life is about right now.

The six remaining cards should all be about your future time. It's your life line; the choices are all yours. This gives you a chance to imagine just how you'd like your future to shape up.

When you've got the ten cards done, punch holes in them and hang them in your room. Take a look at them from time to time. What you've done is take a look at your life, right now. In six months, you may feel very differently. Remember, as time moves along, changes move right along too — they are bound to happen.

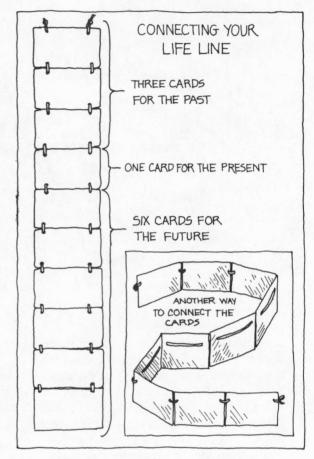

CONNECTING YOUR LIFE LINE

THREE CARDS FOR THE PAST

ONE CARD FOR THE PRESENT

SIX CARDS FOR THE FUTURE

ANOTHER WAY TO CONNECT THE CARDS

Conclusion
The Past 757 Million Years on Earth

DO YOU KNOW HOW OLD THE EARTH IS? SCIENTISTS TODAY THINK
THAT THE EARTH, LIKE EVERYTHING ELSE IN THE SOLAR SYSTEM,
WAS FORMED FROM A HUGE CLOUD OF MATERIAL FLOATING IN SPACE,
AND THIS HAPPENED ABOUT FOUR AND A HALF BILLION YEARS AGO.

THAT'S SUCH AN ENORMOUS AMOUNT OF TIME, IT'S JUST NOT POSSIBLE
TO FATHOM IT. BUT YOU CAN TRY. READ THIS ANNOUNCEMENT.

AN INCREDIBLE MOVIE! A FANTASTIC EPIC!

THE PAST 757 MILLION YEARS

IT'S AN AMAZING EXPERIENCE!

ON EARTH

NEVER BEFORE SHOWN TO ANYONE!

HERE'S YOUR CHANCE! DON'T MISS IT!

It has taken the past 757 million years to make this phenomenal film. The film was shot from another planet, using an exceptional supertelephoto lens. It wasn't made like an ordinary movie at the usual twenty-four pictures a second. Oh, no, this movie isn't ordinary in any way. It was made with a time-lapse camera that snapped one picture every year. Remember, the camera did this each year for the past 757 million years.

When you see this unusual film, you'll be seeing twenty-four years of the earth's history on the screen in each second. That's because the movie will be run at the normal projector speed of twenty-four frames a second. It's a jam-packed experience.

This movie is quite an epic. The entire movie will run continuously from beginning to end. It will start on midnight of New Year's Eve, and it will run without stopping until midnight of the next New Year's Eve. That's one entire nonstop year of film. You'll see almost two million years of history every day. Have you ever had an opportunity like this? Don't pass it up!

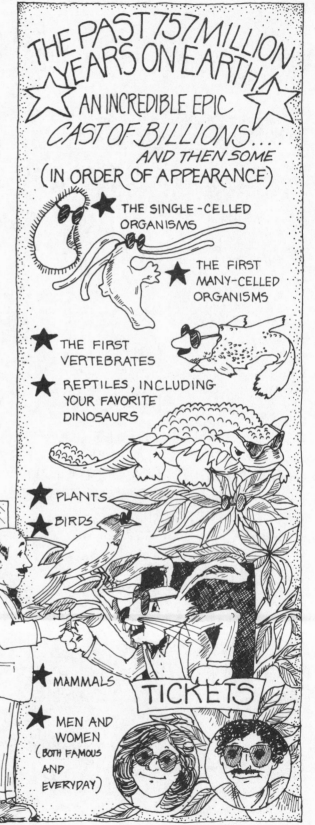